Growing Up
With Doris...

And Still Alive
to Tell the Tale

Leslie A. Breen

Cover Art: Courtesy of Megan Breen
Patchwork Quilt made by Sarah Breen

Other books by Leslie A. Breen: *Cooking with Doris B.*
www.CookingWithDorisB.com

ISBN: 978-0-9842447-0-6

Printed in the United States of America

10 9 8 7 6 5 4 3 2 1

LAB Publications
505 Paradise Rd. #118
Swampscott, MA, 01907-1958
labreen@comcast.net
www.LABPublications.com

Acknolwedgments

I would like to thank all my friends that were an intricate part of my dream becoming a reality.

Shannon Phelan, you had to endure reading and editing the first draft, a giant run on sentence.

Samantha (Taymore) Dunn, for doing the final edit the week before your wedding.

Lynne Schueler, for all those weekends spent formatting both books.

Megan Breen, for your creativity, cover design, artwork, and being a wonderful daughter.

Doris, who on a daily basis told me to keep following my heart and my dreams would come true.

Finally, my husband Kevin. You were there for the highs and the lows. It has been a long journey, but we did it together. Love you!

Prologue

Who is Doris Gloria Silva-Brown? That woman would be my mother. Doris was born on September 26, 1924 in Peabody, Massachusetts. She was the first and only child of immigrant parents Joseph and Teodolinda Silva. At the time of her birth, her parents shared a three-room tenement with two other couples. The day she was born was the proudest day of my grandfather's life. Dreaming about being a father had finally become a reality at the age of 36 years. He took his new daughter, gently swaddled her in a blanket and placed her in the open top dresser drawer as her bed.

Doris is 100% Azorean Portuguese and is very proud of her heritage. If those of you reading this story lack geographical knowledge, the Azores are composed of a group of nine tiny Islands. They are a possession of Portugal located 972 miles directly west of the capital of Lisbon and 2,000 miles off the East Coast of the United States. You could say that they lay smack dab in the middle of the Atlantic Ocean. In 1993, I had the joy of visiting the island of Gracoisa, with my family and Doris.

Laboring for over 40 years in the leather industry, her parents lived a simple life. They never owned a car or had a telephone in their four-room apartment. My grandfather was very influential in his daughter's life. He instilled his values of family first, always give to those who have less than you, provide your children love and an education and you will live a good life. Joseph was a man of few words; he lived by example.

Doris moved into her current two-family home when she was only three months old and spent the next 18 years living within that five-block radius. Being an only child, her early years were spent praying for a baby brother or sister that never came. Unfortunately for Doris, her mother Teodolinda felt she had met all her wifely obligations and motherly duties when she gave birth to Doris. My grandmother had to care for multiple siblings when she was a child and never really enjoyed a childhood of her own. These issues surrounding children made her a cold woman when it came to expressing her emotions. It would be safe to call Doris a Daddy's girl.

Education was the number one priority in Doris' life since her own father, whom she worshiped, was illiterate. The first school she attended was the local Carroll Grammar School and later graduated from Peabody High School, Class of 1942. World War II was a backdrop for her teen years. Doris' contribution to the war effort was a job in a light bulb factory as a laborer on an assembly line. It cemented the importance of education for Doris. She made up her mind early in life that she would not spend 40 years in a factory like her parents did. Once the war ended, she went into Boston to a business school and became a bookkeeper.

If you asked Doris what she wanted to be when she grew up, it was always the same thing, she never wavered: a mother. Her dream was to marry the love of her life and have as many babies as possible. She told me stories about the man she loved, her soul mate. He was a G.I, straight home from the war. His name was

George and he was a good friend of her cousin Manny, who lived down in Rhode Island. He would take her on dates in an old 1936 Ford that had no heat. In the dead of winter she would wrap the ends of her fur coat under her feet and cuddle up to him as close as she could. In 1966, when she saw him again for the first time in over 20 years he bragged that his 1936 Ford had the best heater in town. Doris looked confused until he admitted he would turn the heat off, so she would be intentionally cold and have to snuggle up to him for body heat. But unfortunately in 1947 he had come into a few thousand dollars and suddenly a girl said she was pregnant with his child. George did the honorable thing and married her.

The irony was that this woman had pretended to be pregnant and later staged an elaborate miscarriage. Her plan was to get George to marry her and get all his money. It had all been a lie. This woman had denied Doris her soul mate and George was trapped in a loveless marriage. Doris went on with her life and on June 26, 1949, married my father. It turned out he was a rebound husband, not her true love.

She moved downstairs to the first-floor apartment of her parents' home, and everything was wonderful. Except there was just one problem, Doris couldn't get pregnant. She had been trying for almost two years, taking her temperature and timing her menstrual cycles, and no baby. The doctors told her she would never give birth to any children of her own.

I came to learn from my mother at a young age that the word "NEVER" does not exist in her vocabulary. Never was just a synonym that meant find another solution to the problem. If the doctors said she would never conceive and give birth to her own child, she would adopt one. This woman was determined to be a mother and have a baby through whatever means necessary, so she immediately started the adoption procedure through Catholic Charities. On June 22, 1954, she became the proud mother of a beautiful baby boy, named after my father. Was it a coincidence or an omen that he shared the same birthday with my father?

Weeks after the miracle of becoming a mother, Doris was rushing down the stairs from her mother's apartment when she lost her footing and tumbled down seven stairs. Aside from bumps and bruises she was fine until later that evening. Suddenly she began having vaginal bleeding. Doris had actually been pregnant and suffered a miscarriage. This loss of a child would have put some women into a deep depression, but not my mother. Doris saw it as another miracle. Imagine her delight to realize that she could indeed conceive a baby. All those educated doctors had been wrong. My mother did indeed get pregnant again, giving birth to me in 1957 and again in 1962 to my baby brother.

This story, if you haven't already guessed, is about the love of my life, my mother. We affectionately referred to her as Doráss when we reached our teen years. Through these stories, I hope to give you a glimpse of what it was like growing up in the 60's and 70's with Doris. As a testament to my mother, life living with Doris was never dull or boring and was always an adventure.

Witch Doctor Doris

Growing up, I never realized that we didn't have a lot of money and that going to the doctor was expensive. We had our yearly physicals, vaccinations and the occasional sick visit to rule out strep throat. Doris had almost an obsession that a Strep throat untreated could lead to Rheumatic fever, cardiac complications and possible death. When she was a child, before the era of antibiotics, many children had died from the complications of Strep infection.

I know we had medical insurance, good old Blue Cross and Blue Shield, but back in the 1960's there weren't any HMOs (Health Maintenance Organizations) and primary care physicians were a concept that was far into the future. Insurances only covered hospital stays, emergency room visits and elective surgeries. These circumstances are what probably led to Doris being accused of practicing medicine without a license, by our pediatrician. She was never actually formally charged, but he would threaten her on many occasions over the years.

My earliest memory of a doctor/Pediatrician was Dr. McGlynn. He was in his late 40's and had eight children of his own. He was the old fashioned, black medical bag, house call making doctor, that you would see in a Norman Rockwell painting. He was available to his patients and their families twenty four hours a day, seven days a week. That dedication was what probably led to his premature death at the young age of 52.

My baby brother Toney had his share of illness and accidents before the young age of ten. He was a frail infant and toddler plagued with abscess ear infections. He also seemed to be accident prone with broken bones and major accidents that almost took his life on more than one occasion. One particular Saturday morning I was the catalyst to his almost fatal accident.

My cousin Gabby and I had planned a Saturday morning shopping trip. In 1967 you could still find a bus that passed at the end of my street and took you to downtown Salem, Massachusetts. It is the historic city where they had the infamous witch trials. Women were hunted down, tried and convicted of practicing black magic mainly because they were different. The fate they endured was either to be burned at the stake or hung. Neither method was one that I would have chosen to end someone's life even if they were supposed to be convicted criminals.

Salem was about a mile from my house and we would go to an old Five and Dime department store, called Almys. It was 3 levels: Basement; household good's, linens and small appliances. Main level; Woman's clothing, cosmetics and jewelry. Second level; men's and children's clothing. I don't think I ever went upstairs unless I just wanted to ride the escalator. We could try on clothes, hats, and my favorite, jewelry that we could never afford to buy. The older sales women looked as though they had been there from the 1940s and I think they actually had.

The real treat was to have lunch at the old fashioned lunch counter tucked into the front corner of the store. You could sit on red stools that swiveled 360 degrees and looked like mushroom caps. Or, if you were looking for sophistication there were a few booths, also upholstered in red vinyl. The tables were a gray and white Formica that looked like puffy cloud formations. It had the traditional soda fountain serving drinks like root beer floats with vanilla ice cream, the famous Raspberry Lime Ricky, or a Cherry Coke. The special of the day would be a grilled cheese, tuna fish or grilled hot dog, complete with chips and a coke for 75 cents.

This particular morning my baby brother Toney, who was almost five years old, was being more cranky than usual. He was chasing me around the small apartment crying "I want to go to Salem, I want to go too." There was no way that I was having him tag along with Gabby and me. It was a big girl shopping day and he was not coming no matter how much he cried. But just to guarantee that scenario, I ran out the front door and up the hill to meet Gabby, leaving Toney yelling behind me.

I was gone for about four hours and the entire time I was oblivious as to what had transpired at home. Toney, who had a temper, came running after me. He was approximately three feet tall and with an outstretched arm just made it to the storm door handle. This was 1967 and storm doors were comprised of 2 panels of plate glass. It was not tempered or shatter proof glass used in the windshields of today. I have been told that he was running and his hand slipped and his arm went through the plate glass door.

What happened next was bedlam. Toney let out a blood curdling scream that had all the neighbors, including Doris, out into the street. Doris got to him first and his right arm was dangling at his side and the blood was actually spurting out as his heart beat. Toney had severed his radial artery and he was bleeding to death. The next door neighbor was home, got his car and sped Doris and Toney to Salem hospital.

The entire ride Doris says that all she remembered is apply steady pressure with her hand wrapped around his tiny wrist. As a girl scout leader she had learned a few things about first aid and knew she also had to release the tourniquet every few minutes for a few seconds. Doris had managed to limit the blood loss and when she ran through the emergency room doors carrying her baby, the doctor was able to clamp the wound. It looked like everything was going to be alright until the doctor said that Toney needed emergency surgery, if he was going to survive. Toney threw up his arm, the clamps came flying off and he actually lost more blood in the Hospital Emergency Room than he did on the ride there.

My baby brother did survive, but he did a lot of damage not only to the severed radial artery, but also to the nerves and tendons in his wrist. He came very close to having his hand amputated that day. When I got home that afternoon and Junior told me where Toney and my mother were I was hysterical. I can remember crying until I finally fell asleep. From that day on going to Salem lost its appeal. I think I knew deep down it wasn't totally my fault, but I did contribute to the events that day. I will always hold some guilt and remorse about what happened to my baby brother that Saturday.

One rainy Saturday afternoon, Doris let my cousin Gabby, my brothers and I play cards in our new travel trailer, parked in our driveway. We made believe that it was our own special club house. Toney was being your typical annoying three year old when he kept whining that he wanted to go up into his bunk bed. After endless no's I finally broke down and tossed him up into the bunk. He was playing, opening and closing the blue privacy curtains when there was a dull thud. We all looked over and there was Toney lying lifeless on the tiny white vinyl floor. We all froze. My mother was going to kill me because I was the big sister and I was supposed to be taking care of him.

What happened next was like a movie, and I was an actor, it wasn't real. I remember yelling as I ran from the trailer toward the house, "Mom, Mom come quickly, it's Toney, he is hurt badly." Before I reached the backdoor she was past me and already in the trailer. He lay there motionless. Doris swept him into her arms and ran to the next door neighbor's house. He was always home and had a car. The whole time I remember saying "I am so sorry, I am so sorry." Today it remains one of the most terrifying times in my life. I honestly thought my brother was dead.

Thankfully he regained consciousness about thirty seconds after they pulled away in the car. He came home later that night with a diagnosis of a moderate concussion. This time there were no broken bones. We all took turns keeping him awake for the first twenty four hours, until he was out of potential danger. I never knew why it is so important not to let a person sleep after they have suffered a concussion. Maybe it was felt if they slept they could die and you wouldn't realize until it was too late. But Toney survived yet another near death experience.

The Antibiotic

As far back as my memory goes, my baby brother Toney was always sick. I remember my mother and grandmother taking turns walking the floors all night, and he would not stop crying. Toney had over 50 abscess ears before he reached two years old. On one of the rare visits to the doctor's office, Dr. McGlynn lanced another abscess ear to relieve the pain and pressure. (Lancing is not an accepted practice today because of the fear of infection.) The doctor then gave him another antibiotic to prevent such complications.

In the 1960s, there were only a few antibiotics to choose from, not like the arsenals of super drugs that exist today. So, Doris took my brother home and left him with my grandmother while she went to fill the prescription at our neighborhood pharmacy. This was years before the era of the mega chain drug stores like CVS and Walgreens. They were small, independently owned and operated usually by the one and only pharmacist.

The problem was that my mother tore up the new prescription. Instead, she took an old medicine bottle that had refills and filled an antibiotic from an ear specialist Toney had previously seen in Boston. Doris had no formal medical training. The prescriptions did not come with any written packet insert about side effects. Yet without any reason she changed the medicine. Why would Doris do a thing like that?

She walked into the drug store and behind the counter stood her friend Mr. Weber. With all Toney's problems, my mother and Mr. Weber were becoming fast friends. He was older than Doris, in his early fifties, just graying at the temples and very distinguished. He stood over six feet tall and was always dressed in a white, double breasted, starched bib type jacket. It was the kind of coat that doctors like Dr. Kildare and Dr. Ben Casey wore in their latest medical TV dramas. Always there was a plain brass name tag over his heart that read, Mr. Robert Weber, registered Pharmacist.

Doris returned with the new antibiotic and all seemed to be going well. Three days had passed when suddenly Toney developed a temperature of 104 degrees. He was delirious, his pajamas soaked in sweat and Doris knew there was no time to waste. My parents drove him to the local emergency room, and I remember my grandmother sat on our front stairs crying for hours. The feared infection had occurred, and it was now throughout his tiny body. Toney was septic.

Our local hospital was not equipped to handle such a sick child, so he was immediately transferred to Boston's Children's Hospital, via ambulance. Toney was placed in the intensive care unit. He just laid there for three days, and Doris never left his side. His stainless steel crib resembled a tiny 3×3 foot jail cell.

His color was pale and his body listless. Two I.V. bottles hung above his head, tubes placed carefully into his tiny veins. They were the crucial antibiotics and fluids he needed if there was any chance of him surviving. Doris just sat there thinking she had killed her baby.

Suddenly, after three long agonizing days and nights the tiny hand that Doris had never released, the lifeline to her baby, gave her a gentle squeeze. Doris looked up, and there was Toney smiling at her. She told us as she was crying over her mask, Toney looked up at her and said "I want a hamburger and French fries, and Mommy sing Pinocchio." It was as though he had just woken from an afternoon nap instead of a semi-conscious state. The fever had broken and the worst was over. The specialist told my mother that she should thank her pediatrician. If he had not prescribed the combination of Penicillin and Sulfa that Toney had taken the three days prior to admission, he would have died.

From behind she felt a presence, then a hand on her shoulder. When she turned around, there were the kind eyes of Dr. McGlynn peeking above his surgical mask. He had driven into Boston to see how Toney was doing and heard the entire exchange. The masks over their faces hid their expressions, but their eyes communicated it all. He knew that he had not been the one who saved Toney's life. It was Doris. To this day, she doesn't know why she changed the medicine, what possessed her that day but is still so grateful to God that she did.

Over the years, Doris has done things and had premonitions or dreams that she has followed without knowing why. There was always a favorable outcome. I also seemed to have inherited this sixth sense and always listen to that little voice inside my heart, just like my mother always did.

Hooked on the Fence

Growing up, I was not what you would call a petite, feminine little girl. "Chub Bette" might be a more descriptive term, since I was 40 inches tall, and weighed 88 pounds in the first grade. My fellow classmates came up with the nickname "Pounds" when we studied the abbreviations for weights and measures. Someone realized that my initials were lb, thus pounds. Also having two brothers and a predominately male neighborhood didn't help my appearance. I was your typical Tom Boy in every way.

After school, my activities included football, baseball, hockey and my favorite, army. On TV at this time were shows like *Rat Patrol* and *Combat*, and we all wanted to emulate these TV heroes. We would gather our play machine guns and make up opposing units, and we would fight until someone won the battle and ultimately the war.

Our street was an eclectic mix of one and two-family homes, but the street that ran parallel to ours was not yet developed. Two of the lots were just mounds of dirt sprouting various wild grasses and towering at least 20 feet high. These became our battlefields, appropriately named "Lamb Chop" and "Pork Chop." The boys named the hills, and I think they named them for some battle from World War II or the Korean War since Vietnam was just beginning.

One day we were defending Lamb Chop, which was on the side of the street that backed up to our house. Things were not going well for my platoon. It was retreat or face capture by the enemy, so we ran. Retreat meant scaling three to four 4-foot tall chain link fences that divided our backyards.

I put my white Ked sneaker into an opening in the chain link to boost myself up and over, but getting my large derriere over wasn't that easy. The next thing I remember, I was impaled on the fence. I had slipped, and the top two inches of the rusted fence were embedded into my soft fleshy thigh. At first I think I was in shock because it was surreal. I didn't feel any pain. Then I heard my brother screaming for help. When I looked down, all I saw was bright red blood running down my leg and dripping all over my new white Ked sneakers.

I am not sure how they did it, but my older brother who was about 13 years old at the time, and his friend lifted me off the fence and carried me home. Doris was just coming out the front door, as were most of the parents in the neighborhood who had heard the ear piercing screams. My mother told them to take me into the bathroom and sit me on the toilet. She was cool and calm as she gathered ice, peroxide, and gauze that she needed to take care of me. The entire time they were telling her what had transpired.

Doris knew she had to stop the bleeding and clean the wound thoroughly. She placed some ice in a face cloth and applied pressure to the area. Thank God it had been in the center of my leg and not my groin, near the femoral artery. Once it stopped bleeding she could see it was approximately four inches long and one-half inch deep and one-quarter inch wide. I really should have had stitches, but Doris had these things called butterflies. They were shaped like dumbbells, one inch in length, quarter inch wide and resembled band-aids, but they had string-like reinforcements that ran through them. They were almost impossible to tear once applied and as difficult to remove.

Doris was a big fan of peroxide, and she proceeded to pour almost an entire quart bottle into my open wound. She did have the compassion to pop two Tylenol into my mouth the minute I stopped crying. When she felt it was sufficiently clean and I was up to date with my Tetanus vaccine, it was time to close up the wound. While my brother helped to hold the edges of my flesh and adipose tissue together, she carefully applied the paper sutures. They were the precursors to steri strips that are used in surgery today. Next, she applied the staple of her medical bag, good old bacitracin ointment. She finished it off with a large clean gauze pad dressing held on with old-fashioned white medical tape.

I was and still am amazed that Doris always seemed to know what to do. My doctor today says that my scar looks better than if I had had the thick sutures that they used in the 60's. She was ahead of her time because now they use super glue and steri strips to close up wounds. I would compare my mother's technique and results with any legitimate doctor's work from the 1960's or today.

The Mole

The year I turned thirteen Doris all of a sudden became fixated on skin. Up until this time her major medical concern for her children was getting a strep infection and ending up with rheumatic heart. Now she was looking us all over to find anything that resembled a potential fatal skin cancer. All freckles, blemishes and discoloration from a pinpoint to the size of an eraser were inspected.

It must have been during this time when the surgeon general and health department began their campaign on using sun tan lotion to prevent sun burns and their potential dire consequences. I can remember my two older cousins, a natural blonde and red head, with alabaster skin sitting in our yard lathered in baby oil mixed with a drop of iodine. They actually had the metal reflectors that they held under their chins to get an even facial tan. I also remember my mother soaking face clothes in white vinegar and ice. She would apply cold compresses all over their red, burnt bodies. The vinegar took the sting out of the burn and the ice helped to prevent blisters.

During all our trips to the beach, the only sun protection I remember was sitting under the beach umbrella while we ate lunch. I never remember having any protective skin lotion applied before going to the beach to prevent anything. Otherwise it was hours frolicking in the sand and surf. If Doris did think that our shoulders might be getting a little pink, on went one of my father's oversized cotton T-shirts. This was her version of the first sun blocking fabric.

I vaguely remember the television ads for Coppertone. The little girl approximately 2 years old having her bathing suit bottom tugged down by a dog, revealing her tan lines. The ad was always referring to sun tan oil to get a deep brown tan. Never an ad for sun screen products to prevent sun burns and future skin damage.

All of Doris' children were fortunate that they had inherited her olive complexion and not my father's white Irish skin. That is not to say that we would occasionally get the rare sun burn especially on our cheeks, nose and shoulders. Normally we would tan and by the end of the summer would have a reddish brown glow. My board straight hair with natural henna highlights hung down to my waist. I parted it straight down the middle and wore the occasional headband across my forehead. By the time I returned to school in September I looked like an Indian. Today the politically correct term would be Native American.

As was often the case with my mother she would read something in a newspaper or magazine and had just enough knowledge to make her dangerous. Doris never seemed to get the whole picture. This time I did give her credit for being proactive and doing everything she could to protect her kid's future health, and prevent skin cancer.

So one night as I was getting out of the shower she decided to do a skin check. There was a knock on the bathroom door and she yelled, "Leslie I want to see if you have any weird moles that we should show Dr. Rizzo, at your physical." I knew my mother. Doris was not going to rest until she could see for herself that no potential fatal skin cancers lurked on her only daughter's body. So in she came.

While modestly holding the towel around my chubby pubescent body, Doris began the inspection. Holding a piece of white paper, actually the inside of a used envelope, and pen in hand she started at my head and went down writing the exact location and approximate size of any imperfections. Okay, she had one. On the inner aspect of my left upper arm was a raised, dark brown mole. She was almost excited that she had found one. The article specified the danger of moles located in places that could be irritated over the years. These moles had a greater probability of turning cancerous. So the fact that it rubbed against my chest was not good.

Doris concluded the exam with the foot inspection. Knowing what I know now there had to be some mention of Melanoma in the article because the foot exam was very through. She looked at the soles, webbing between my toes and both sides of each foot. Then came the gasp. "What? What? What's wrong?" I asked. Up until the gasp, I attributed the whole thing to one of her compulsions to prevent anything bad from happening to her children. Now I was scared. What did she find?

Have you ever tried to look at the side of your foot? It takes some contortion skills. I suggest first to be in a sitting position. Bring your foot back bending at the knee, twist it outward at the ankle, and look down past your hip. Sounds easy enough unless you're standing up, damp and clinging to a towel, it can be deadly.

I didn't care anymore about modesty I just wanted to see what grotesque thing had Doris gasping. I sat on the open toilet seat and in one jerking movement was staring down at the culprit. There was a 2cm, raised blackish brown nevus. The texture was rough but it was perfectly circular, thank God. Why hadn't I seen it before? I had been taking showers for the past few years, no tub baths. When did it appear?

Off I went the next week for my annual physical with doctor Rizzo, our new Pediatrician. He also specialized in adolescent medicine, which was a plus for Doris since she now had two adolescents. Doris chose our new doctor because she had gone to high school with him and it was the only reference he needed.

The office was in a three story, dark gray, Georgian style home off of Main Street in Peabody. The house was divided down the middle and the left side door led upstairs to the office suite. Reaching the landing at the top of the stairs, you were faced with two options, left or right. Left led to three small rooms. The first was no bigger than a closet where the receptionist sat at a small desk. She answered the phone and checked patients in. The nurse's station was directly behind, in the converted kitchen that doubled as a laboratory. Off of the nurses area was the only exam room.

The closed door to the right was the doctor's private office. This also opened directly into the only exam room, from the opposite side. It reminded me of the early drive thru McDonalds. At the landing give the order to the receptionist and pay, go to the exam room to wait, and finally through to the doctor's office for the meal pick up.

Once again Doris had been right. Dr. Rizzo apparently had read the same information about potential skin cancers, but I am sure his article was in the American Journal of Medicine and not Ladies Home Journal. Both of these moles had to go. So my mother's favorite surgeon, Dr. Jones was called. A date to have them removed was arranged before we even left the office. Doris' feeling was the quicker I could be rid of this potential lethal nevus the better. Then she was not the one who had to go through the procedure.

I never had anything happen to me involving medical procedures with the exception of throat cultures, yearly TB tests and blood draws. I was naïve. How does one remove a mole? So I made a big mistake and asked Doris. It was Doris after all that started the whole thing. She had done the reading so she must know how it was done. That was my first mistake.

In the late 1960's early 1970's there were no referrals. My doctor called the surgeon and told him what I had over the phone. They actually talked to each other, no faxes or emails. I had a 10 minute visit with the surgeon to look at the moles and 4 days later I am walking into the outpatient surgical center at Salem Hospital. It seemed to happen overnight. Doris had come into my room the night before the surgery and explained what would happen in the morning.

First I had to be NPO, nothing to eat after midnight, so I had an empty stomach the next day. This was a precaution in case I was nervous; they didn't want me to vomit during the procedure. Her explanation was that they would spray a numbing solution over the area and then burn the mole off like a wart. It might sting a little, but she was sure they would give me something for the discomfort, wrong.

At the surgi-center I was led into a dressing area by a nurse no more than five foot tall and just as wide. Her shoulder length hair was bleached blond and was partially covered by a nurse's cap. She never smiled and acted like a prison matron that I had seen in a movie. She said in a flat voice "Go into the dressing room, remove everything from the waist down." "Everything?" I asked with a voice that was barely a whisper. "You can keep your panties on but hurry and put on the Johnnie with the opening in the back." She barked.

Out I came and I was motioned to climb up onto the stainless steel table that was positioned in the center of this sterile room. The light above it was so bright it was blinding if you looked directly at it. It was shaped like a flying saucer that I had seen on an episode of The Twilight Zone, with an alien invasion. Now I was starting to get scared. What was going to happen next I thought?

Now in came Dr. Jones in scrubs, covered by a yellow gown tied in the back. He was a little man about five foot five inches tall and had small hands with nicely manicured nails. I know now how important it is to pick a surgeon with little skilled hands because the incision will also be smaller. For some reason I thought about Dr Rizzo's hands. They weren't large and his fingers weren't overly long but they were shaped like stubby cigars.

Finally the doctor spoke. "Lie on your right side so I can see your left foot, and get into the proper position." At the same time my friendly nurse came back into the room with a surgical gown over her white nurse's uniform. Why were they covered by surgical gowns? Doris said it was a piece of cake, a little spray to numb the area and one two three and it was burnt off. Why suddenly did I not believe my mothers words. Doris had never lied to me and I trusted her with my life. The reality was that she did not know what she was talking about and had been clueless about this procedure.

The nurse placed a pillow under my head but the table was still very hard and uncomfortable. Now wearing plastic gloves the nurse uncovered this little table and I saw what was hiding under the drape. "Oh My God," was all I could think. There were various bottles of liquid, needles of various sizes and there was a scalpel. They were going to cut it off and I was going to be awake. I now understood about the no food so you don't vomit precautions. At that moment I can assure you if I had eaten, it would have come up.

I felt that I had entered the Twilight Zone. They didn't say anything to me except not to move my foot. I was frozen in fear until the surgeon drew up some of the liquid into a syringe then fear became terror. What was he going to do with that 4 inch needle? Within seconds I found out.

The doctor only said "I am going to numb your foot." He injected the bottom of my foot in 3 places and then the sides. It was as though I had just stepped on a rail road spike. I got a totally new appreciation for what Jesus endured on the cross. As I laid there helpless, clenching my fists and grinding my teeth all I could do was think, when I get out of here I am going to kill Doris. I am going to kill her. Her words echoed in my mind, burn it off, a little sting, it is a piece of cake.

This little mole on the side of my foot was not superficial. It had a core that went 2 cm into my foot. Dr. Jones had to make the incision larger and deeper than he had thought. It was a crater that would have to heal slowly from the inside out. I would not be able to bear any weight until it was completely healed. This meant crutches, which lasted almost six months.

When it was all over the doctor went out into the waiting room and told Doris the problems that they had run into. Meanwhile the nurse actually helped me to get dressed. They fitted me with my crutches, a quick lesson on walking and I was ready to go home, with Doris. When they opened the door my mother was standing there waiting. I was going to yell at her but then I saw her face. There was anguish and signs she had been crying. I realized that she was sharing my pain. Doris had told me what she honestly thought was going to happen. I had believed her because she had never lied to me and she hadn't this time. This was once again an instance of Doris only having half of the puzzle, reading part of the story and assuming about the second half. She made it up to me. I was spoiled until the foot was healed and I was back to 100%.

When I finally went back to have the mole removed from my underarm, I asked the surgeon what this one entailed. He assured me it would not be as painful because the foot is the most sensitive area on the body. It turned out not to be that bad. I knew what to expect and this mole wasn't as deep. I learned a lesson that day: only ask Doris how to cook and leave everything else to the professionals.

Dr. Doris – Alias Dr. Ruth

Doris always told us stories about herself and growing up in the 1940's, when most of the boys in her class of 1942 were away fighting in Europe or the South Pacific during World War II. I would hear about the soldiers coming home for leave and looking for a "good time." Through these stories, Doris would instill her values and beliefs about a woman's reputation. She always tried to instill through funny stories how important self worth, dignity and virginity were. Most of these stories revolved around me holding onto my virginity until marriage since I was her only daughter.

As a teenager, Doris was only 5 feet, 2 inches tall, with a slight build and weighed only 98 pounds, soaking wet. Her jet-black hair would only grow down to her shoulders in length, but outward it was wild and frizzy. From pictures I have seen, I would describe her as attractive with a great big smile that was contagious. Since she had already endured living with my con-trolling grandmother for over 18 years, her humorous outgoing personality was ingrained in her for self preservation. Doris could tell jokes and stories that would have her audience in hysterics. She was known by all as a good time, only not the definition that most of the GI's were expecting, when they only had a few days of leave before going back to battle.

Doris would go on a lot of blind dates during this time in her life. A friend's boyfriend would come home on leave, and she would double date with his friend. Sometimes she would know them and other times it would be a total stranger. To protect her-self, Doris would weave a three-inch hatpin somewhere on her person. Rumor was she would dip it in water so it was rusted and would cause lockjaw if used on some unsuspecting, horny GI. My own daughters would need an automatic weapon to keep most boys inline today. Things have definitely changed over the years, but a girl's reputation is still the most important thing she will ever own.

Leslie's Coming Out

My older brother had four friends all through his childhood, and one went to Harvard on a football scholarship. The summer after his freshman year, he brought home one of his dorm mates, Darren from California. Darren's mother was origi-nally from Peabody, and he was going to spend the summer with his grandmother on the family homestead. Mrs. O'Brien lived six streets and 25 houses away from ours in the wealthier section of town. The neighborhood was a little more upper middle class; all the houses were one-family center-entry colonials. The sides of the street were lined with oaks and maple trees growing tall and full over the road, giving it a canopy effect.

Darren's parents lived in Beverly Hills, and his father was some type of movie executive. His younger sister Stephanie was joining him for the summer from boarding school in England. Doris had the hardest time understanding how someone could send their daughter away for high school and not see their child for over a year. My mother was dreading her children going away to college. Eighteen years was such a short time to have your children, to intentionally send them away baffled her. Doris would not even send us away to overnight camp, and the fact that she didn't have the money had nothing to do with it.

Darren had already become a permanent fixture in our home by the time Stephanie arrived. Her age was supposedly 16 years, but she presented herself as a woman of 25 with the street smarts to go with it. Her clothing could only be described as shabby chic. My look on the other hand was more hand-me-downs from big green trash bags. I was so naive that I thought everyone shopped for their wardrobe from plastic bags. If things were too big they were saved, too small they were passed on to someone else. Underwear was always bought new from the Sears catalogue every September; even Doris drew the line at hand-me-down underwear.

I call that summer "my coming out" and not of the closet. I was a very studious, conservative person, and a little on the chubby side, a combination that did not make me Miss Popularity. I didn't smoke cigarettes or do any drugs of any kind, and didn't even drink alcohol. I think Miss Goody Too Shoes about sums up my reputation at Bishop Fenwick High School, but that was all about to change. Doris had always been a big believer that we learn from our mistakes. Sometimes you have to learn the hard way and not take your mother's word for things. Mother hen was always there, but she let me spread my wings a little that summer.

Stephanie had been in Peabody for less than two weeks, and she was already dating one of the most popular boys in my school.

He was someone I had gone to school with since first grade and he had a reputation of doing drugs. In 1973, we were talking about marijuana and alcohol comprising the majority of drug use.

Half way between my house and my high school, there was an ice cream stand that was the local adolescent hang out. It was on one corner, of a plain red brick building that housed four retail stores. There was a pharmacy at the opposite end, a barber shop and small variety store. The entire front facade was glass and you went up to one window to order and the other to pick up. To make it easy, two signs hung from the ceiling on silver chains to make sure you didn't make any mistakes.

At the time a one scoop "baby cone" as it was called was 8 cents. Also they served a traditional banana split made in a 4×8-inch cardboard bowl. It was a banana, sliced lengthwise and laid in the bottom, with 9 scoops of ice cream and your choice of flavors. Finally the toppings, hot fudge, pineapple and strawberries all covered in a pile of fresh whipped cream, crushed walnuts and a cherry on top. It was a 2,000 calorie feast.

One summer evening, Stephanie asked me to accompany her to a party that she was invited to. Doris gave me her permission to go and be home by 11:30 P.M. I was 16 years old, and I was thinking house party, but what did I know.

I left my house wearing navy blue shorts, an oversized Patriots T-shirt and white leather sandals. At the time, I thought I looked hot. Stephanie, on the other hand, was wearing a long gauzy teal green skirt, sexy white halter-top and high-heeled gold metallic sandals. Her hair was sun-streaked with various shades of blonde and blew freely around her face. She reminded me of a gypsy, and all that was lacking to complete the look were large gold hoop earrings dangling from her ears.

When we got to the ice cream stand, we crossed the street and walked through the abandoned bank parking lot. Where the hell were we going? I had lived here my entire life and didn't know what lurked behind the innocent bank facade. Stephanie led me by the hand down a path through the bushes and trees, and suddenly there was a clearing and the smell of the ocean. I had known that there was land behind the bank and that it was part of the unused portion of the cemetery, but we were almost at the ocean. How far had we walked?

I was so taken aback by my surroundings that I failed to hear the gasps that were coming from the small groups of teenage girls and boys. All of a sudden all you could hear was, "Brown, Brown, what is she doing here?" You would have thought the Virgin Mother had just been seen from the reactions I was getting. Stephanie couldn't fathom that my being there could have had such an effect on everyone. What she didn't realize was that the reaction was because no one could believe that I could know Stephanie. We were like day and night. Doris had always said, "Tell me who your friends are, and I'll tell you what you are." Apparently, this particular group of teenagers also believed in this principle.

Stephanie had developed a reputation for being very worldly and overly friendly. I, on the other hand, was the chubby one, a straight A student, and hung around with the nerds and geeks. Suddenly all that changed. Sixteen years of who and what I was, wiped out by my association with one girl. There were "bad boy types" hovering all around me. I suddenly had the image of a pack of wolves eyeing fresh meat, and I was the prey. In the time span of 15 minutes, I was popular. All those fantasies of boys wanting to date me were coming true, only it didn't feel right in my gut. I felt a sudden sensation of panic. I was in way over my head, and I didn't know what to do.

I was standing there, and it was so dark I couldn't see where Stephanie was, and I thought I must have been dreaming. Was I hearing bells? No, they were sirens and within seconds Peabody's finest had broken through the trees in all directions. We were surrounded by six police officers. There was no place to run.

Everyone stood still, and there was an eerie silence. The boy standing next to me whispered, "Now we're screwed." My short life flashed before me. If I got arrested, there was my nursing career gone before it started. Suddenly I remembered Doris' mantra over and over: "Get arrested, enjoy the vacation, because I can't afford to bail you out." Please don't arrest us.

I was convinced it couldn't get any worse when I heard one officer say, "Miss Brown, come over here right now." Why me? I was a good girl. All I wanted was to see how the other half lived. He led me to the farthest side of the clearing, and I got a look at his face. No, not my crossing guard for eight years and my mother's high school classmate. He looked me straight in the eyes and said, "Does your mother know where you are? She is going to kill you when she finds out." I explained what had happened, and I might have fibbed a little. The police decided to just confiscate the alcohol, and since no pot was found, give everyone a warning. The group opinion was that I would rat them out to save myself and when I didn't, I was a hero.

When I got home two hours early, Doris knew something had gone wrong. I had always been honest with her because she found out anyway, so why take the chance? I explained how all these kids that I grew up with suddenly wanted to take me out. I'll never forget the four questions she asked me that night. "Leslie, what has changed about you in the last two weeks? Did you suddenly turn into a skinny fashion model? Did you have a personality overhaul? Did you acquire a new friend?"

I answered "A new friend." Her reply was "good grasshopper," using the phrase from David Carradine's new TV show *Kung Fu*. Doris could have told me not to go with Stephanie because the boys would think I was easy through association. Instead, my mother knew it was better for me to learn for myself. I was upset because I wanted to be popular and have a boyfriend. I realized that I just wasn't ready to put out for some oversexed 16-year-old boy who would screw anything that had an orifice. I wanted to wait until a boy liked me and would not pressure me to do something I wasn't ready to do.

Stephanie continued to come to the house, and we would do things together, just no parties. When she was leaving to go back to school in England, she told me how lucky I was to have Doris as my mother. I already knew that, and I felt bad for her. I don't think I could have gone over a year and not have seen my mother. I was grateful for the fact that we were poor and that my family didn't have the option or finances to send me away.

I have two daughters, and I have tried to guide them and let them make their own mistakes. They know I am always there for them and that they can tell me anything. I'll just yell and scream, and then their calm dad can handle it. But one thing they know I won't do, is post bail. "You get arrested, have a nice vacation." Some things are still the same.

The Apple

Doris would repeat many sayings that she had heard over the years. She felt a picture was worth a thousand words. One I will never forget was, "A French kiss is an upper persuasion to a lower invasion." Also, "Boys are after one thing sex and notches on their belts." I went around for the longest time actually looking at belts wondering how many girls that boy had conquered. Her sayings for my brothers were, "It's not you I don't trust, it's your hormones." "Remember, the girl you lay could be the mother of my grandchild and could you live with that?" "Take precautions, put a rubber on it." "No piece of tail is worth a piece of mind." Doris was never one to mince words.

Doris was and still is a fabulous cook. Every Sunday around one o'clock, we would sit down as a family and have an elaborate family dinner, so Sunday evenings we would have a light supper. One of our favorites would be fried dough.

She would put it together when everyone was watching the Red Sox or Patriots game, just flour, water, sugar and yeast. It was always placed in a crock bowl, with a dinner plate on top as a lid. Then the place of honor, near the radiator to ensure warmth and guarantee it wouldn't catch cold. She always covered it with the same two old gray and pink wool baby blankets. At 7 P.M. it was ready and time to start frying the dough.

There would be maple syrup, butter, powdered sugar or sugar cinnamon to put on the mouth-watering creations. Doris vowed to use nothing but King Arthur flour, and she has been using it for over 60 years. The family on any given Sunday could be at least 8–10 people. My older brother had at least five childhood friends that practically lived with us, or I should say ate with us, on a regular basis. One night after eating the fried dough and drinking a gallon of milk, Doris had a surprise for my brother's friends.

I was sitting at the table, and people were just about to clean up when Doris asked everyone to stay seated. My brother's friends were 17 years old give or take, and they all thought she had made one of her special desserts. They were so wrong. Doris had gone into the refrigerator and pulled out a large shiny red delicious apple and proceeded to shine it with a clean dishtowel. She didn't say anything but kept rubbing until it was glistening. Then Paul asked, "So what are you going to do, Mrs. Brown?" Everyone knew that Doris liked to play practical jokes, and they were all confused and suspicious.

The five boys sitting around the table were Philip, Randy, Junior, Jeff and finally, poor Paul. My mother told them they were going to play a game, and the idea was to take a bite of the apple and pass it on to the person to your left. I could see the concerned look on Paul's face at being last. Doris handed the apple to Philip. He took a huge bite and passed it to Randy, and he did the same.

When the apple got to Paul, all the shinny red skin had been eaten off. Paul turned the apple around by the ends, but there was no side that he could take a bite that wasn't already bitten by someone else or turning brown. Paul said, "Mrs. Brown, I'm not taking a bite of this dirty old apple core." Doris replied, "Exactly, a shiny red apple that goes around from boy to boy becomes an old dirty apple core. Just like a woman that goes from man to man, she starts out young and beautiful then ends up a dirty old whore."

They all just sat there. No one said anything for a few minutes until Doris broke the silence with, "Think about that when you think you're getting lucky. If she is putting out for you, how many guys were there before you? You might get more than you bargained for." Paul confessed many years later that he was making out with a girl he had just met that night, and all he could see was the dirty old apple core, and he had to stop. As Doris says, "A picture is worth a thousand words."

Sex 101

Doris had never really given me the entire sex talk. In Girl Scouts, she handed me this pretty pink booklet titled; "Now you're going to be a woman." The troupe disbanded before the next series came out. I often wondered what color and title that one would have had. Maybe red and titled; "Now you're really going to be a woman" or "Time to get married and have sex." Maybe "It's time you get laid" or "The Art of Lovemaking." These titles would never have made it past the Girl Scouts of America. It was just a thought.

I do remember the night that I learned where babies really come from. I was 12, and my two older cousins, Gabby, age 15 and Lucy, age 13, gave me the true unabridged story. We were at my house having a sleepover, and the subject of sex came up. I can assure you it wasn't by me since I was still playing with my Barbie dolls. Lucy had witnessed her parents doing the deed and felt it was her duty to explain it to me in great detail. Like every adolescent, I could never picture my parents having sex. It must have just been those two times to create my younger brother and me, right? Today, when my two girls see their father and I kissing, my Megan will wave her hand over her eyes and says "NO visual, NO visual." I guess some things never change, even after 35 years.

Growing up, I was not the most beautiful teenager. I had a slight weight problem, and the word that always came to mind when describing me was attractive, never pretty or cute, and definitely not petite. Once I had asked Doris, "Mom, am I pretty? Or am I ugly?" She replied, "You're pretty ugly." It took me a while to figure out what she meant because I don't even think she knew why she said it, other than it just sounded funny. Later in life, Doris kept trying to apologize for that statement. I think it was the only time she said something that hurt another person, even though it was unintentional.

Let's just say the boys were not knocking down my door for dates. It also could have something to do with the fact that Doris had threatened castration for anyone who touched her only daughter. Not a combination that was conducive to being popular. When I entered college however I lost 30 pounds, developed breasts and had a 36-24-36 body to die for. I started to have some self-confidence, and I thought I looked beautiful. Apparently some men felt the same way. I was no longer referred to as Brown's little sister by my brother's college friends, I was HOT.

One of my brother's friends, Paul, was also one of my best friends. He was adopted from Catholic Charities a few months after my brother. We joked that he could have been my big brother, and our relationship always remained platonic. Paul graduated from Salem State College the year I completed my freshman term in their nursing program. He had a good friend and classmate named Sean. He was a little older, 28, divorced and a Vietnam vet. He was definitely a lot worldlier than I was at 19. He was also graduating with his business degree.

Paul invited me to join him at all the Senior Week activities as his "date." Senior Week included nightly parties, all leading to the senior dance and graduation day. Day one started at a beer bash at an old bar called Sweeney's Gay Nineties. When you walked in, you could smell stale beer, cigarettes and peanuts. The floors were old worn wooden planks covered with the remnants of old-fashioned roasted peanut shells. Its walls were covered in old barn board, and a second floor balcony ran around the entire perimeter of the building. A giant stage at the far end of the first floor, with a live band made up the décor. The only problem with this band was that it was a marching band that was stationary. It even included a tuba player who had to cover the opening of his instrument with screen mesh to prevent people from throwing peanut shells into it. Not your typical disco club of 1976.

Sean was already at the club when Paul and I arrived. Two couples, two single guys and Sean made up Paul's group of friends for the week. All of a sudden, this guy was showing me an undue amount of attention. He sat next to me at our table, poured my beers all night, and finally he asked me to dance. I loved and still do love to dance. Unfortunately, dancing was not one of Paul's strong points. His friend on the other hand could dance, John Travolta, Saturday Night Fever type dancing. It didn't hurt that he was handsome with the most beautiful emerald green eyes with long black lashes that curled up to his eyebrows, bedroom eyes. Sean also made no secret that his intention was to dance, drink and by the end of the night, get me into his bed for a roll in the hay. I think he had actually used the term "get laid," which was not very romantic.

I grew up on Doris Day and Rock Hudson movies. Where was the courtship, candlelit dinners, long sexy kisses, then marriage and sex? All those sayings that Doris had drilled into me over the years came fluttering back. "If you give the milk for free, they never buy the cow." "A man will say and do anything to get into your pants." "Do you think he really loves you? He only met you three hours ago." "You don't think it is your personality they're after, do you?" Why couldn't it be all right to just have sex? Because I was raised by Doris and after 19 years, I believed what she had taught me.

The week progressed, and we went to a giant luau at Kahlun, a giant Chinese Polynesian restaurant on Route1 in Saugus, Massachusetts. The scenery included a thirty-foot tall, wooden Tiki God, and drinks with fruit and umbrellas, instead of beer and peanuts. The location had changed, but the scenario was the same. Always Paul's five friends, Sean and I dancing and drinking and me always going straight home, alone. This continued for five days and ended with the commencement ceremony. Everyone gathered after the graduation for a large party at Paul's house with friends, family, Sean, Doris and me.

It surprised me that I had survived the week of sexual advances, drinking and dancing. It was funny because I had always wanted someone to want me, but not for just casual sex. I wanted someone I could fall in love with and love me back, an authentic relationship. I remembered Doris' stories about if a man loves you, he always has your interest as his first priority and no piece of tail is worth your piece of mind. It was branded into my soul that the most important gift that I can give to a man is myself, my body. Today, more than when I was growing up, girls have such low self esteem that they give their bodies away like a stick of chewing gum.

Paul lived in my neighborhood in the top two floors of a three story duplex that his father owned. The apartment door opened directly into a modest 12×15 foot living room. To the left was a door leading to the dining room at the front of the house and small kitchen to the back. All the furniture had been placed against the perimeter walls and folding chairs were added for more seating. I drove Doris with me, and she was so proud of Paul since she considered him her other son. Doris would joke if there had been any slight change of fate, she could have adopted Paul, and Junior could have been a Dube instead of a Brown.

Doris arrived and wasted no time going directly to her favorite room in any house: the kitchen. When we talked about getting married, she would tell me to pick one room in my house to excel in and concentrate on it. Her joke was that she chose the kitchen using the phrase "The way to a man's heart is through his stomach." Later in life she felt the bedroom might have been a better choice. Planted on the last folding chair in the kitchen and just inches from the living room door, Doris was ready to party. What I failed to realize was that Sean and I were seated on the other side of the wall and only one foot of plaster separated Doris from him.

Sean was a determined man, and he gave it his best effort to make one more attempt at conquering me. He was trying all of his best lines. He could teach me a few things; he was older and more experienced. We had a lot fun together this past week, why not keep the fun happening. I was finding this amusing. No one had ever tried so hard to get me into his bed, and I just kept saying no. He was relentless. What he did not realize was that Doris was also enjoying his antics from around the corner in the other room.

Doris had been listening and making jokes to her kitchen audience about that poor girl being subjected to such bullshit. What she was not aware of was that I was that intended victim. Her comments ranged from the "wolf in the hen house" jokes to "if he was so desperate to get laid, go to Union St. in Lynn and pick up a hooker and leave this poor coed alone." Then Sean made his catastrophic mistake and said, "Come on, Leslie, I promise it will be a night you will never forget." As it turned out, it probably went down as a night he never forgot, as he uttered those famous last words.

The possessed Portuguese mother from hell was out of her chair and in his face in ten seconds. I hadn't even had enough time to give him an answer to his proposal. Doris said, "Excuse me." Sean turned around and said, "Who the hell are you?" Doris replied, "Her mother and your worst nightmare." Doris started on a tirade. "I have been listening to your half-ass lines for the past 20 minutes feeling sorry for the poor girl that was being subjected to such an asshole. Then I realized my poor daughter was your intended victim." Unfortunately, Sean had never had the pleasure of meeting my mother, but those who knew her were in search of Paul to calm her down and prevent any bodily injuries to Sean.

While this exchange was all going on, I felt like I was having an out of body experience. I watched this 5 foot 2 inch woman take on a 5 foot 11 inch guy, and all I could think was that someone better protect him fast or he was in danger of losing the family jewels. Then he made his fatal mistake and uttered in her face, "This is none of your business lady. Your daughter is a big girl and can take care of herself, so get lost." I thought Doris was going to have to be restrained. Her face was getting scarlet, and the veins in her neck were pulsating when Paul entered the room. It was too late. She had her finger in Sean's chest, looked him straight in the eyes and said for the entire house to hear, "If you need to get laid so bad, why don't you poke out a knot from the knotty pine paneling over there and go to town, but your time harassing my daughter is over."

I'm not sure how Paul was able to get between the two of them and how he kept Sean from saying another word. He convinced him to cut his losses and try his routine on some other single coed and stay clear of me. Paul made him aware of Doris' threats over the years that anyone who tried to touch her daughter was going to find himself castrated. Paul had experienced the wrath of Doris on previous occasions. Everyone there knew that I was never going to give it up for Sean, but they also found his pursuit comical. Even Paul on one occasion had tried his best stuff on me, only to have both of us laughing senseless. We decided that best friends would have to do. We did joke on occasion that if we were old and never married, maybe we could get together. Deep down we knew the marriage would only last through the honeymoon, so we didn't lose the deposit on the trip.

I never saw Sean again until 20 years later at Paul's 40th birthday party. He was with his second wife and he looked frumpy and overweight with a receding hairline. One thing he still possessed were those dreamy bedroom eyes. I introduced myself, and he immediately asked if my mother was there. I assured him he was safe. Doris was a little older, and now that I was married with two daughters, she was much less aggressive toward potential wolves. We laughed and introduced each other to our current spouses. Then in front of 10 people, my husband and his wife, Sean announced that I was the only girl that he could not lure to his bed. I was in shock. My husband chuckled and replied, "Well, I guess I should be grateful that you didn't say she had banged you and the entire debate team." We laughed, but Paul had a concerned look that he might have to defend Sean again over my honor. I looked at Kevin, and he had this smirk on his face. He had a little secret of his own; he knew that he was the one and only one who had ever taken me to bed.

Chef Doris

I'm not sure when Doris learned to cook, but she tells stories of having to start the soup when she was eight years old. Since both of her parents worked and she was an only child, it was left up to her to get the evening meal started. She started with a large pan of water and threw in a few pieces of beef and vegetables. To this day, she can't remember if she even peeled the vegetables, but the beating she received she does remember. Apparently, when Teodolinda arrived home and removed the lid on the pot to check on the soup, it resembled "turds floating in water," according to Doris. But somewhere from age eight through my childhood, she became an outstanding cook.

Today as I try to create healthy tasty meals for my family I am still in awe of her culinary talent. Doris could take the least expensive cuts of meats, add rice, vegetables and her father's wine and create a meal that could pass in a 5 star restaurant. The one and only thing she lacked was presentation. Her only criteria for a superior meal was taste, be inexpensive and most important, it had to be cooked and served in one pan. She hated doing dishes.

We used to spend our summers at a campground in Well's Beach, Maine. We had a small 17-foot travel trailer with an 8×10-foot canvas room attached to the outside. One summer Doris found out that there were free delicacies if you were willing to work for them. She loved anything that was edible that came out of the ocean. We had been on a tight budget during those summer months when Doris discovered a crustacean called mussels. They were a cousin of the clam, had blackish purple iridescent shells and clung to the undersides of rocks at low tide. Doris had cooked steamers so what was so different.

Doris and her kids went down to the beach at low tide and went along the rock jetty. We were all dressed for action. The uniform of the day for the kids was bathing suits covered by a T shirt and our oldest worn out sneakers. There were no water shoes in those days just canvas Keds. Doris was wearing her classic peddle pushers, or as we refer to them today, Capri's. My mother was never to be caught out in public in a bathing suit of any kind.

The jetty was about 25 feet out from the beach and the ocean floor was rocky, Doris didn't want any injuries. There were clumps of these strange creatures everywhere and you just had to gently pull them off their perch. Some caution was required due to the snails and other sea barnacles' that were part of the sea life. When we had filled our large lobster pot and multiple sand pails we headed home to start the cooking. Doris knew to only keep the ones whose shells were tightly closed. We started an assembly line of rinsing and scrubbing as many of the barnacles off as possible. When she was convinced that all the sand and unidentifiable things were gone, there was a decision to be made. How do you cook them?

She had cooked steamers in the lobster pot with just some water and white wine. But she didn't have a clue to what the meat inside looked like or for that matter what it tasted like. The owner of the trailer park had lived on the ocean his entire 60 years and he had never eaten a mussel. According to Doris you could never go wrong with alcohol and fresh veggies. She layered 4 inches of the shelled creatures, ringlets of green peppers and onions, fresh garlic and kept repeating it until it was to the top. Finally a bottle of an inexpensive red wine was poured over the creation, topped off with the pot lid. With care and brute strength the pot was carefully placed on the grate over the glowing fire pit. Wait for the concoction to come to a boil, 20 minutes of cooking time and Voila.

Well, to say it was superb, outstanding, delicious was an understatement. It fit all of Doris' criteria of what constituted a good meal. Inexpensive (it was free), flavor, (red wine and garlic), and it could be served in the pot it was cooked in, (centered on the picnic table with a large ladle and bring your own bowls). Who knew how tasty they were and a great source of protein. The entire trailer park got to taste their first mussel.

Who knew that a gourmet meal was just down the road and free for the taking? But a few years later everyone found out our secret and the town started to regulate mussel picking. There was a town ordinance that you needed to be a resident and get a permit for recreational clam and mussel digging. This did not stop Doris. The trailer park owner also loved his mussels so once a summer we would go with him, necessary legal documentation in hand, and we would all pig out on Doris' mussels.

Beef Heart And Rice

When I was young, I didn't realize we were poor. I thought all families played "Find the piece of chicken in the chicken and rice" game. Ninety percent of our meals were meat flavored, but actual meat was rarely in the ingredient list.

We spent our summers in Maine. My father came up on the weekends, so Monday through Friday we walked everywhere or hitched a ride with other campers. At that time, we only owned one car, a lime green Rambler station wagon. The meals during the week were meals on a shoestring budget. Doris would joke that one of her favorite creations was "shit on a shingle." Doris was never short on four letter words. One thing my mother could do was take the ingredients from her pantry and refrigerator and make them taste like a gourmet meal.

One particular week, funds were low and Doris went to the grocery store with the family next door who happened to have a car. Her challenge was to create a dinner from her very last dollar, so we could make it until Dad arrived with the next paycheck the following day. The chosen menu was beef and rice. At one point we ate so much Uncle Ben's converted rice I thought we might have some ancient Chinese lineage. That particular week, we had my youngest brother's best friend Chris staying with us. Chris was one of 11 children and a very finicky eater, bologna and cheese on white bread being his staple food.

Doris arrived and went directly into the trailer and began cooking dinner. She had purchased a beef heart that weighed just over a pound. It was a great source of protein but it required a little more preparation to be able to eat it. She had to meticulously cut out all the veins and make sure she cut out the areas that would be tough to chew even after it simmered for hours. Completing her task she was left with a bowl of cubed pieces of beef. Then there was the simmering in a wine sauce, add the rice to cook and it was finished.

Doris was very prompt and dinner was always served at 5 P.M. sharp. Out came the gigantic stainless steel pot right onto the picnic table. Doris must have missed something in Emily Post about how to set a proper table. I was probably 16 years old when I realized serving pieces actually existed. Other people didn't place the meal on the table in the same pot it was cooked in. People had bowls and platters that actually matched the dinnerware and were actually used just for serving the food, not cooking it. Doris hated doing dishes more than anything in life. The idea of one pot to cook, serve and clean seemed logical to her.

Doris' beef and rice was delicious, and the pot was scraped clean. Suddenly the next-door neighbor she'd gone shopping with stopped by to see how everyone liked the beef heart. The look of confusion slowly grew on Chris' face, and he turned to Doris and squeaked, "Mrs. Brown, what was that beef? It was beef, right?" His face was getting green around the edges, and his eyes were pleading for the answer he wanted to hear. Doris, cool as could be, replied, "It was beef. It came from a cow. It just happened to be the heart, diced up into tiny little pieces."

The word poor Chris had dreaded hearing was "heart." So it was true, he had been duped into eating cow heart. It was though his insides went into instant revolt. He sprinted for the bathhouse, not able to make it in time. I guess my family was used to organ meats. Gizzards, liver and chicken necks were fairly common-place and delicious when sautéed in wine sauce combined with our staple, rice.

From that day on, Chris played it safe with bologna and cheese or peanut butter and jelly on white bread. To this day, he is still my brother's best friend and frequents Doris' house on special occasions. Even though he has matured and has expanded his palate, you can always see him looking suspiciously at anything Doris serves him with rice.

Giant Cream Puff

I always felt that Doris never fully grew out of her prankster ways. She loved a good practical joke. She would never intentionally humiliate or hurt anyone. Her jokes were always in good taste. Her intention was to bring out our human frailties and show us that no one in the world is perfect. Everyone is human and makes mistakes, but some mistakes are more amusing than others. Her intention was to get us to laugh at ourselves and not take ourselves too seriously. The ultimate goal was to always learn from your mistakes, grow and go forward.

All throughout grammar school, I had a crush on a boy named Peter. I would do anything for him to like me or talk to me. One thing Peter loved was when my mother made her famous oatmeal or Tollhouse cookies. He knew I liked him and would deny him nothing, so he always managed to get one of my cookies. More than cookies, the tasty treat he would kill for was one of Doris' homemade cream puffs.

Doris was a master at the creation of cream puff shells. They were always fluffy and delicious even though they were rarely perfectly round. We would play "What does the cream puff look like" before they were filled. Was it a duck, a dog, or a plane? You never knew what shape they would take. Doris would literally plop the dough on the cookie sheet with no real pattern and wait to see how they transformed in the oven.

This is where she came up with the plan for Peter's special birthday present. She would create the cream puff of all cream puffs. The biggest, most perfect confection filled with luscious vanilla cream. Doris' usual method for filling the cream puffs, when they were two inches in diameter, was to cut a small piece off the top, scoop out any excess dough, and then fill them with a few teaspoons of cream and replace the top. Peter's cream puff, however, measured a remarkable 12 inches wide and 8 inches high. It was golden yellow and perfectly formed in every way. So what was the joke? It involved a cake-decorating syringe with a long point so the cream filling could be injected right into the center of the puff, all two pounds of rich, smooth vanilla pudding.

Dear R—

Hope I didn't hog the book too long. I assume there are others hoping to read it.

All's well — as are you + yours also —

Love
mom S X

The next day, I went to school and promised Peter a surprise for his birthday lunch. My mother had received permission from the sisters to deliver the surprise the next day at 11:30 A.M. Doris also thought that Peter's mother might like to be included in the surprise, so she invited her along.

The long awaited birthday arrived and promptly at 11:30 A.M. in walked Doris, Peter's mother and Sister Superior. In Doris' arms, she cradled a 14-inch diameter hatbox, wrapped in silver paper (actually aluminum foil) with a large green bow on top. All the children in the class started to whisper as my secret infatuation with Peter became broadcast news. My fellow classmates stared chanting, "Leslie loves Peter, Leslie loves Peter." I could feel the color rising up into my face. I looked at Doris, my eyes begging her to do something. She took charge of the class and got their attention as she made the announcement, "Everyone quiet or you won't get to see what is in the box." It worked.

The gift from Mrs. Brown was placed in front of Peter on his desk. Slowly, he unwrapped it, opened the lid and peered into the box. He gasped and then screamed, "It's the biggest cream puff I've ever seen!" It could have been in the Guinness Book of World Records. Peter looked confused. How does one begin to eat such an enormous confection? The answer is very slowly and very carefully. Peter placed his hands on either side of the puff and carefully removed it from its place of honor in the box. Surveying the crowd, and with all 52 students in the class watching intently, he slowly brought it towards his mouth. The kids and Sister Agnes all gathered closer as no one wanted to miss the moment of impact. It was as though it was happening in slow motion. The puff moved closer and closer until finally he opened his mouth as wide as he possibly could and contact was made.

His jaw muscles contracted; his teeth started to pierce the outer layers of the shell when suddenly . . . KABOOM, we had detonation. The pressure of his mouth closing in on the shell increased the pressure inside. The creamy goodness had nowhere to go except out, in every direction. It was like watching the world's largest zit being popped. Everyone was paralyzed. There was cream everywhere. On the desks, on Sister Agnes' habit, on his mother, and of course, Peter, and any other student caught in the blast zone. Silence engulfed the room until Peter swallowed his first bite and confirmed, "It's the best cream puff I've ever eaten!" The room exploded with laughter. It was like a food fight in reverse. People were grabbing cream from every surface and licking the place clean. Well, almost clean since everyone had to stay for a massive soap and water cleanup after school.

I graduated from St. Thomas School in 1971 and the one thing that everyone still recalled was the day when the biggest cream puff in history blew up in Sister Agnes' class.

The Blizzard

I attended a Catholic grammar school that was run by the Sisters of Notre Dame Order. The Catholic Church, being male dominated, gave the priests of the parish new cars, dinners out and a housekeeper. The nuns, on the other hand lived a life of poverty. They cooked for themselves, had no access to a car and never enjoyed a dinner out. Something about this inequality didn't sit well with Doris. Seeing the disparity between the priests and nuns, she devised a plan.

St. Thomas Parish had a mothers' club, at a time when most women were stay at home moms and career women were a thing of the future. These women would get together once a month and run bake sales and bazaars to fundraise for the school. At that time, it only cost $20 per child to go to the school if you were a parish member. Such a deal!

Doris got the idea that the nuns were getting a raw deal. They had to cook for themselves, and since most of them had no training, they were not very good at it. She came up with the idea that each mother would put in a dollar a month towards the "cooking fund," and Doris would cater a four-course meal once a month for the sisters. Doris told me that she recently found her notebook where she tallied the costs and expenditures for the meals putting her bookkeeping skills to work even then. The average meal for the nine sisters, with extras was about $16.

As inspiration for her meals, Doris would choose a country, such at Italy, Portugal or Greece, and write a story based on the food they would eat and where everything originated. Always included were a few of her famous jokes, all cleaned up and appropriate for the sisters' virgin ears. The menu included one to two appetizers, salad, one to two main courses (so they had a choice) and a surprise dessert. This monthly event became the highlight of the sisters' social lives.

When the day of the monthly meal had arrived, there was one big problem: it was February and we were in the middle of a good old nor'easter blizzard. It had started snowing at 10 A.M. and by 3 P.M., the road and the hill we lived at the bottom of was covered in 12 inches of fresh white powder. The visibility was almost zero. One of the only things Doris feared was driving in the snow. Like the postal service, Doris was determined to deliver the meal. Neither snow nor sleet would keep her from her mission. The problem was how would she get there?

The solution came to her out of the blue as she looked over at our sleeping German-Shepard-Alaskan-Malamute dog named Scrapper. He stood about 3 feet tall, weighed 74 pounds and was perfect for the job. What Scrapper liked more than anything was to run in the snow. So the plan was to deliver the food the old Eskimo way, on a "dog sled."

My brother was immediately sent to the garage to get the two large Flexible Flyer sleds, and to clear a path from the front door, down the stairs to the street. While Junior was outside battling the elements of nature, Doris started the indoor preparation. She took out the two summer coolers from the basement. In the blue cooler for cold, she placed a layer of ice cubes along the bottom and stacked all the ingredients for the antipasto. Since it was to be served on a large platter she decided to assemble it at the convent.

Doris packed the red cooler for the hot food. She poured boiling water into it, swirled it around for a few minutes, and then emptied it in order to get the inside hot before she put in the food. The outside temperature was hovering around 16 degrees Fahrenheit. In went the trays of lasagna, meatballs, sausage and peppers, all divided by metal cookie sheets that also helped to keep in the heat. The surprise dessert had already been created and assembled in a Tupperware cake carrier. Since it could be exposed to the cold temperatures, she decided to just tie it onto the sled as is.

Thank God for Doris that her dog adored the snow and was strong enough to pull the sled and all the cargo. Scrapper had already been lashed to the first sled using a makeshift harness Junior created using small pieces of rope. The two coolers were carefully carried to the lead sled and tied down with old fashioned white cotton clothes line rope. Bungee cords were still someone's future dream and ticket to the Millionaire entrepreneur club. Behind the coolers in the place of honor was the cake carrier with the dessert. Adding to the excitement was the fact that the phone lines were dead and we had no way of letting the sisters know we were coming.

The second sled was used for human transport of my baby brother Toney. Junior pulled that sled with a six-foot rope that he draped over his head and held in front of his chest. My job was to carry the snow shovel in case the entrance to the convent was blocked and the stairs had to be cleared. We all headed up the mountain like a caravan. Doris, guiding Scrapper with a small flashlight, led the way. By now the snow was coming down sideways and visibility was two feet at the most. We were wearing so many layers of clothing that we could hardly walk and the only things exposed were our eyes. Between the fridged temperatures and the wet snow, it felt like little needles pricking any exposed skin. My brothers were in the middle and I made up the caboose, and our adventure was off.

We had to cover a straight shot of approximately 300 yards from our front door to the front door of the convent. The roads were barren. There was not a vehicle in site. In the distance, we could see the faint lights of the convent through the windows. As we got closer, we could make out a face in the front window peering out into the snow. Sister Martha was the designated lookout. The rest of the nuns were in the chapel praying that the meal would arrive. They had such faith in Doris no one had planned an alternative for dinner. Sister Martha let out the call, and all the sisters ran to the kitchen door to let us in from the cold.

It took 15 minutes to clear a path to the door and shovel off the stairs. Once all the coolers and the cake carrier were safely on the kitchen counter, we had to wait a few minutes for Sister Superior to make a decision. She had to grant a special dispensation to allow a wet, tired Scrapper into the convent. She realized that Scrapper was the answer to their prayer, "Give Mrs. Brown the ability to safely deliver our meal, Amen." Scrapper was allowed into the kitchen and wrapped in a warm cotton towel.

Once in the kitchen, we were stripped of our wet clothing and the food was removed from the coolers. The secret dessert was kept a secret and placed into the refrigerator. Then Doris began the tradition of reading her story about the meal. In this case, it was "So you're going to Italy." Doris described the origin of their lasagna, who created the first meatball and all the ingredients in the antipasto. This antipasto was a meal in itself with mixed greens, tuna, shrimp, prosciutto ham, provolone cheese, marinated black and green olives and roasted red peppers. It was almost obscene, like culinary foreplay for the meal to come. Doris assembled it onto the large oval platter she had brought from home. Now it was time to eat. Since this had not been the normal delivery drop and run, the sisters broke with tradition and asked us to join them for dinner. They were already excited by the meal, and Doris assured them that the dessert would be sinful.

After the meal, it was time to reveal the dessert. Doris had created a six-layer yellow pound cake soaked in apricot brandy, layered and covered in fresh whipped cream laced with still more apricot brandy, and decorated on the top with slivers of dried apricots. One problem that Doris had not taken into account on our journey was the 65 degree incline of the hill leading to the convent and the inevitable shifting of the cake off its platter. When she opened the lid of the cake carrier, she was the one that got the surprise. The cake had had a major transformation. It had slid on and off the plate and adhered to the sides of the carrier. She just barely managed to curtail her four-letter words. She quickly adapted by turning the carrier upside down and using the bowl-like lid to create a makeshift apricot truffle. Instead of serving beautiful slices, Doris scooped hefty portions into bowls and we used spoons instead of forks.

The blizzard lasted eighteen hours and no one left his or her home for about two days. When Doris received the thank you note from the sisters for their wonderful trip to Italy, it was truly a thank you. Doris had made so much food that they were able to eat off her one meal for four days. Also, Sister Superior added a P.S. at the end telling Doris that two of the sisters had to be put to bed after indulging in two helpings of the apricot dream.

She cooked for the sisters for another four years and never missed a month. The nunhood changed over this time, and the sisters wore shorter habits and were allowed their own car so they could shop and be more self-sufficient. A new pastor came to the church and confiscated all the bankbooks of the clubs, including the mothers' club cooking fund. It was the beginning of the end for St. Thomas Parish. In 2005, the parish was slated to be closed due to financial deficits within the Boston Arch Diesis. To date it has not been sold, but sits as a reminder for my family of all the time spent at mass, receiving the sacraments and the marriages that once took place there, including mine and Doris'.

P.I. Doris

My mother always had a sense of adventure. She was a stay-at-home mom until my older brother Junior went to a Catholic boys' high school in 1968. Doris returned to work full time so that she could finance her children's private education. Education was always Doris' number one priority, no matter what she had to do or how much she had to sacrifice.

She worked hard for her money as a full-time bookkeeper in a local leather factory. It was a male dominated work environment and she suffered financially over the years due to it. Doris made less money with her associate degree than the males who were floor supervisors and had only a high school diploma or less. But she was willing to endure these injustices so her children could have a better life. No one was going to deprive her children of what was theirs. Doris was like the lioness protecting her cubs and she demonstrated it one Wednesday afternoon in April 1970.

Bike Thieves

Toney, eight years old at the time, had received his first new bicycle for his birthday in January, and the weather was finally permitting him to try it out. The snow had melted, so he could ride it outside the garage without fear of injury or road grime. This particular day, I made it home from school early and thought I would take a little spin around the block on the new bike. The bike was magnificent with metallic gold paint, a banana seat and swooping curved handlebars. It was a three-speed with conventional pedal brakes, as well as one hand brake for added safety.

I had just cleared the top of the hill heading home when two boys about 14 years old were blocking my way on the sidewalk. They stopped me under the pretense that they were looking for their friend Joe's house and wanted some help. Since it was a very close neighborhood, I knew all the kids for three-square blocks, and there was no one named Joe. I noticed the boy spoke with an accent and as I pedaled away they switched from speaking English to Portuguese. The last thing I heard, as I rode away, was "That's a great-looking bike." What they didn't know was that I spoke and understood Portuguese. I returned the bike back to the garage, wiped all evidence of my clandestine ride and went inside to start my homework.

Twenty minutes had passed when I heard my brother Toney screaming from the garage, "MY BIKE! IT'S GONE!" He was crying uncontrollably. In those days we didn't really lock doors and although I had closed the garage door, there wasn't even a way to lock it. I ran to see what he was yelling about and I knew instantly that the two boys I had seen had stolen the bike. I know the law states innocent until proven guilty, but I had them mentally convicted in 30 seconds. My older brother had just arrived home from school, and within minutes the plan was made to call Doris and tell her the bike was gone.

The factory my mother worked at was a half a mile away and she was home in five minutes. She took just enough time to lock the safe and tell her boss where she was going and why. When she arrived, I told her about the two boys I had encountered, and what they had said in Portuguese about the bike. In a flash we were in the car and out on the streets looking for them. My brothers and I went to a parochial school near our home, but the public school was about two blocks away. It was situated next to a park and soccer field, which was a known hangout for most of the Portuguese kids in the neighborhood since they were all into soccer. Doris drove the car into the entrance, jammed the car into park, and jumped out like a crazed woman on a mission. I have to admit I was scared of her, and she was my mother.

The estimated time from me talking to the boys, Toney discovering the robbery and us arriving at the park was about 90 minutes tops. Low and behold there they were standing with a group of older boys when I pointed them out to Doris. She walked right up to them and said, "Did you boys happen to see a gold bike with a banana seat and curved handlebars today?" The two of them looked at me and said, "We didn't see any gold bike with a hand brake." Doris chuckled and replied, "Funny, I didn't say it had a hand brake." It all happened in a split second. She grabbed them both by the arms and the expletives (all in Portuguese) were flying. One of the older boys started to protest because apparently one of her victims was his brother. Doris said, "Fine, you're more than welcome to join us because we're on our way to the police station." He hesitated for about 30 seconds and then ran away.

All crammed into the station wagon, we arrived at the local police station. It was an eye-opening experience. Doris paraded the two would-be bike thieves to the front desk and low and behold, she was a long time friend of the officer on duty. He took

our statements and walked us all into a holding room. Two officers came in to question the boys. All of a sudden there were
tears streaming down the boys' faces and they were unable to
speak any English. This was not a problem since Officer Silva was
also fluent in Portuguese and got the details in their own language. The boys confessed to having stolen the bike, and were
now going to show us where it was.

My brothers, Doris, and I all piled back into the station
wagon, and followed the police cruiser on what turned into a
citywide scavenger hunt. First, we went to the youngest boy's
home and there was the brother from the park and his father. The
father was yelling that his son didn't do anything and didn't steal
any bicycle. Doris decided to take over the conversation. A
woman whose tongue could melt butter when she wanted was
talking like a sailor in Portuguese. She threatened to sue him in
civil court to replace the bike. Doris knew of the family and suggested they might not be here legally and a call to immigration
might be warranted. Within five minutes, Toney's bike tires, handlebars and seat were being extracted from under the front
porch. But where was the frame?

The boy's accomplice in crime, having witnessed the wrath of
Doris came clean fearing what this woman could possibly know
something about his family. He quickly coughed up the location
of the frame. Once again the caravan was off: one police cruiser,
two officers, two scared boys, one irate father and of course,
Doris at the rear. We turned down a small alley behind multiple
leather factories toward a small waterway called the North River.
The stream was used as a dumping ground for tanning chemicals
from the leather industry. In the early seventies, there was no
environmental legislation guarding against water pollution. The
canal was about ten feet wide with fifteen foot tall cement walls
on either side. The water was a greenish black with a shiny

iridescent film on top. The odor bordered between rotten eggs and fresh vomit.

It was starting to get dark, so there was no time to waste. The boy pointed towards the water, and there sticking out of the muck was the fork of the bike with the gold paint glistening in the setting sun. The rest of the bike was submerged and out of sight. The issue became how to get the bike out of the cesspool. The police officer looked at the boy's father and said, "Decide. You or your son?" When I think back, if this had happened in the nineties, I think the father would have sued for police brutality.

The father decided to go in. A rope was tied around his waist and he was lowered over the wall down to the water line. He waded through the muck and extracted the frame from its burial site. We had all the pieces, but the bike was not even close to usable in its present condition.

Doris was not a vindictive person, and she knew neither family had a lot of money. However, she also felt that the boys needed to be taught a lesson that stealing has consequences. Doris' solution was to take it to the place she had purchased it, get an estimate to have it repaired and have the boys split the cost. The boys and father agreed and the ordeal was over . . . so we thought.

Everyone went home with a verbal agreement. Two weeks passed and Toney's bike was returned as good as new at a cost of $45. The frame, which had only been in the river for about 2 hours, had to be sand blasted and repainted due to the corrosion that had already started. Doris dropped off bills to each family for $22.50 and waited for payment. A week passed and Doris felt that was an acceptable amount of time to make restitution. She had to pay for the bike up front and $45 at that time was two weeks rent. She felt she could not wait any longer. She tried calling many times with no response. So the next best thing was a certified, registered letter with return receipt sent in Portuguese. It stated she was to receive the money within 48 hours or she was taking them to small claims court, filing official charges against the two boys at the police station and dropping a dime to immigration.

A miracle occurred. Within two hours, the two fathers were on our porch with cash in hand. Hopefully the boys learned an important lesson that day, "Thou Shall not steal and Thou Shall never steal from Doris' kids."

Milk Money Thieves

When I was in the fourth grade, Doris was the assistant Girl Scout leader of my troop. The meetings were held in the basement gymnasium of the school on Thursday afternoons. Going to parochial school meant wearing those signature uniforms: St. Thomas had navy blue plaid skirts or jumpers with a thin yellow and red line of color running through the material. It was accessorized with white short sleeve-blouses with Peter Pan collars and navy-blue knee socks. The strict rule was that uniforms were to be worn only during school time. So the girls left school at 2:30 and returned by 3:00 in "play clothes" appropriate for the meeting.

As far as the sisters of St. Thomas were concerned, Doris was a living saint. She was the only one I know who had a key to the front door of the school. The school itself was two stories with a split-level entrance that opened between the two floors. The top floor contained the eight classrooms, and the basement contained the bathrooms, gymnasium and principal's office. On this particular day, as Doris and I arrived at the school, three girls were already waiting at the front door. Doris took out her special key, opened the door and let us into the foyer. Once inside, Doris looked up and thought she saw some movement on the upper floor. She told us all to go down to the gymnasium and wait while she proceeded to climb up the stairs. As she slowly walked down the dark corridor, she heard some voices coming from Sister Mary's sixth grade classroom.

All catholic grammar schools were set up exactly the same back then. There were two doors, one at the head of the class and one at the back near the cloakroom. They all had a bank of windows on the far outer wall and a large green chalkboard at the front of the class. The sister's desks were always at the front of the class facing the children and their backs to the chalkboard. The first and second grades were at the far end of the hall and went up to the seventh and eighth grades as you walked toward the front of the building.

When Doris arrived at Sister Mary's classroom door she peaked through the glass panel in the outer door and saw three eleven-year-old boys. They were trying to break into the top desk drawer, where the milk and mission money was kept. It didn't take them long to get what they had come for, and they put the money in their pockets and turned to leave. To their surprise, there was a knock on the door and Doris' face framed in the windowpane. She said, "Hi, boys. Peek-a-boo, I see you!" The three boys froze. They didn't know whether to run or stay, and then Doris opened the door. She told them to empty their pockets onto the desk and get home. Now! They followed her instructions and bolted for the door leaving the money all over the top of the desk.

Doris calmly came down to the meeting. The senior scout leader had already arrived and she conveyed her story. Then she went next door to the convent to tell Sister Superior what she had witnessed. Sister Mary came over to check her room and was able to confirm that all the money was accounted for, but the lock on the drawer was destroyed. Doris gave Sister Superior the names of the three boys and returned to the gym to finish the meeting.

Later that night, there was a knock on our front door and eight young men were standing on our front porch with the alleged thieves among them. The oldest, approximately 18 years old, out of high school and already possessing quite a criminal reputation, stepped forward. He looked Doris right in the eyes and said, "Mrs. Brown, I'm here to tell you that you didn't see anything today." Doris took a step in towards his face and said, "Jeremy, you can tell the police what I didn't see and I'll tell them what I saw. Now get off my porch or we can call the police right now and settle this." They left the porch, but first Jeremy turned around and gave her a look that had my brother and me hiding behind the door. Doris' comment to us after they left was, "Who do those little piss-pots think they are!" And we got ready for bed.

The next morning, my brother didn't want to go to school because he was afraid one of the boys would beat him up. She was having none of it. She told him, "You can't let them think you are afraid." To which he replied, "But I am afraid! " She told us we had done nothing wrong and that you have to stand up for the truth even when you're afraid. So we went to school.

When Junior got to his class, the boy involved in the robbery began to threaten him. "Your mother better keep her mouth shut if she knows what's good for her." Junior was so frozen with fear that he didn't see Sister Superior enter the class with a Peabody police officer, but neither did the thief. When the boy's name was called and he turned around, he was the one with a face full of fear. He and the other boys were escorted from school that day, never to return. The moral of this story is, don't steal from God, especially not when one of His saints is watching.

It didn't quite end there. My mother did testify and gave her statement to the police. The boys involved were expelled from St. Thomas school. About two years later while walking towards the local ice cream parlor, my mother, brothers and I encountered two of the thieves with some of their gang. I use the term "gang" loosely as they were more a bunch of juvenile delinquents. My older brother whispered to Doris, "Mom, look who's coming."

Doris' only comment was to say, "I see them, just keep walking." When we got to the group, the boy who had confronted my mother on our front porch stood aside and said, "Hello, Mrs. Brown. Nice night for a walk." She replied, "Yes, it is Jeremy." We kept right on walking. I was a little nervous, but then I remembered who I was with. My mother Doris was there to protect us. What could possibly go wrong?

The Kidnapping

Doris had been lonely growing up as an only child, with almost all of her relatives from both sides of the family still living in the Azores. In 1932, my grandfather Joseph thought the Great Depression was the end of the world. He felt he would never see his mother or family again, so he booked passage on a steamer and went back to the island of Gracosia with his family. Doris was eight years old when she met all her relatives for the first time in the summer of 1932.

On their arrival, Doris discovered more cousins and relatives than she had ever dreamed of. One week before she arrived a new cousin, Alicia, was born. When she saw Alicia for the first time in the drawer of a bureau (which was her makeshift cradle), it was love at first sight. The baby had big, ice blue eyes and Doris would say the biggest smile you've ever seen. She became the sister Doris never had. During her stay, she cared for the baby and made believe she was her own baby sister.

Doris and family returned to Peabody after three months. They managed to survive the depression and Alicia stayed behind in Graciosa. Alicia's life was far from ideal. Her family was very, very poor, and she was sold to a rich family as a servant when she was only six years old. Her family was unable to feed her and felt this was the best they could do for her. My grandparents had always sent money, clothing and whatever else they could, but it was never enough for the number of relatives they had.

When Doris was in her twenties, she reconnected with Alicia. Things had improved in her life. She was married and had a 3-year-old daughter named Gabby. Her husband was in Canada working construction in hopes of earning enough money to send for them. Their dream had finally come true. As Alicia waited at the one terminal in the tiny airport on Tercadeia for the flight that would reunite her and her husband in Canada, a police officer approached her. Alicia new instantly something terrible had happened. He informed her that they had just received word that her husband had been killed in an industrial accident the day before. While he was hand digging a trench, an unstable bolder rolled back into the hole and crushed his skull. He died instantly.

Alicia started to scream and could not be consoled. She was all alone with her three-year-old daughter and unable to go to Canada. She had to return to Gracosia and wait to see what happened next. This tragedy started Alicia on the road to prolonged mental illness with her first nervous breakdown.

Doris couldn't believe it. She had been planning to go to Toronto to reunite with her long lost cousin/sister. Instead, Doris flew to Toronto (her first time ever in a plane) to arrange for the burial of her cousin's husband. This tragic event threw Doris into action, and she began the process of getting Alicia and her daughter into the United States. It took over two years, but she finally made it happen and her dream of having a sister finally came true.

Alicia was never the same. She was almost child-like when she arrived and had suffered many mental problems during the two-year period. She was easy prey for a less than reputable man named Manny who showed her attention and asked her to marry him within three months of their meeting. It couldn't have possibly had anything to do with the $10,000 insurance settlement for her husband's death. Doris and her mother tried unsuccessfully to prevent the marriage, but, unfortunately in 1962, Alicia married Manny and her real nightmare began.

Manny was the true Devil himself. He was a Peabody native, an only child with rich parents. He had never worked a day in his life. For the first year of their marriage, he treated Alicia and her daughter like princesses, until Alicia gave him a son. Once his son was born, he didn't need her any longer. He had her money and his son, and the only thing he didn't need or want was Alicia and Gabby.

After her son's birth, Alicia went into a deep depression. She no longer bathed or changed her clothing on a regular basis. All she did was sleep. Alicia didn't even take care of her newborn son. His care was left to his paternal grandmother and older sister. From all the things my mother has told me, it sounds like she was suffering from post-partum depression, which was not an accepted psychiatric diagnosis at that time. Manny had her committed to a state mental institution.

The place he sent her was something out of a horror movie. It was only missing a few gargoyles and a perpetual stormy night. From above the complex, it looked like an enormous bat. There was a great tower in the center and the wings stretched out in either direction—the women's wards to the right and men's wards to the left. It was three stories tall and the more dangerous patients were kept in padded cells on the top floor. The whole complex was set atop a hill and was built in the classic Gothic style of the late 1800s in blood red brick. The entire facility was miles away from any residential areas. To keep it segregated the perimeter of the grounds were surrounded by a six foot tall wall of black wrought iron fencing. The only road into the grounds had a foreboding orate Iron Gate that guarded the entrance. It always gave me the feeling that getting in was easy, but I was never sure about getting out.

Doris' hands were tied as to what she could do for Alicia. Manny was her legal husband, and she had no say in her care. But this was all about to change. Alicia was eventually released from the hospital, heavily medicated on Stelazine and Thorazine, and moved back in with her husband. They lived in a small second-floor apartment approximately three blocks from my mother's house. One afternoon, a neighborhood girl came to our door to give my mother a message from little Gabby. She wanted to say goodbye because she and her mother were going to move to Canada. Alicia had one sister who lived with her family in Toronto, and Manny was apparently going to leave mother and daughter with them. It was supposed to be a vacation, but in reality he was trying to rid himself of them by abandoning them in another country.

Doris began to pace in the kitchen asking herself what she could do and how she could stop him. My mother had a bottle of prescription pills her doctor had given her for anxiety during this time with her cousin. She threw one little green and black Librium down her throat, jumped into the car and drove away. I remember sitting there with my grandmother wondering what was going on and where she was going. My biggest fear was that Manny, with his hair trigger temper, would hurt my mother.

She arrived at their apartment only to be told by the next-door neighbor that they had left two hours before in a car packed with luggage. She was too late, or was she? Doris returned home twenty minutes later and told us what had happened. Who could she call to help? The local Police had not previously been helpful. She called the State Police, but they only informed her that it wasn't kidnapping because it was her husband and she had gone willingly. In the early sixties, women were little more than owned possessions by their husbands. Who was left? To this day, Doris doesn't know why or how, but she found herself on the phone to Immigration and the Canadian Mounted Police. The officer felt the story was too crazy not to be true and believed her. She explained to him that Alicia was heavily medicated and was not going of her own free will. Essentially, he was kidnapping her and her daughter with the intention of abandoning them in Canada.

What occurred next was like something out of a movie. When Manny got to the Canadian border, they had a description of his car and license plate. They also had a description of Alicia and her daughter. The officers took Alicia and Gabby into a building and questioned her, but she was so sedated they could not even get a coherent response. Manny was ordered to take his wife and stepdaughter back to Massachusetts and was denied entry into Canada. Doris was far from done. She had won the first battle, but now the war was just beginning.

We were not sure if poor Alicia knew what Manny had planned, but Doris was determined to get her away from him once and for all. Living in Peabody all her life, Doris had many friends/spies who were keeping tabs on Manny's whereabouts and Alicia's condition. One afternoon, Doris parked her car in view of the barbershop where Manny was hanging out. She got out of the car and went into a friend's house with my younger brother in tow. Manny didn't know that she went out the back door, climbed three fences, and arrived at Alicia's apartment from the back stairs. She called to her to come out, but Alicia wouldn't answer. Doris was desperate so she tried another tactic. She said goodbye to her and told her that Manny was taking her back to Canada and leaving her there, and she would never see her baby boy again.

Somewhere in her drug induced haze she knew Doris was telling the truth and she unlocked the apartment door. Doris was not prepared for what she saw. Her beautiful shoulder length auburn hair was greasy and tangled. The body odor was overpowering and her clothing was filthy, covered in food stains. Dark black circles under her eyes were so large it gave her eyes a raccoon effect. Alicia's once rosy cherub cheeks were gaunt and she looked like a person in the end stages of cancer.

Doris was never very athletic, but that day she and Alicia managed to go over three fences and run two and a half blocks until she got her to the safety of our home. Once Alicia was safe, Doris had to run back to her friend's house, coming in again through the back door so Manny wouldn't be suspicious. She walked out the front door with my younger brother in hand, got into the car and drove home. The problem now became how to get little Gabby.

Time was running out. Doris knew it was only a matter of time before Manny went home and found Alicia missing. Doris had a good friend who was an attorney and she called his office. He immediately got a restraining order issued against Manny and called Social Services to the apartment to evaluate the living conditions of mother and daughter. Social Services then accompanied my mother to the grammar school, and reunited little Gabby with her mother. Lastly, the attorney called the chief of the Peabody police department and explained that if there were any interference by the police there would be a full-scale inquiry. He painted the picture of the scandal regarding police officers that ignore the imprisonment of a mother and daughter by her husband. He mentioned the multiple complaints filed against the husband that went uninvestigated by his police officers. He also mentioned that the local newspaper might be interested in the story. So things went smoothly.

Doris wasn't quite finished with Manny. My mother had set up a savings account for Alicia when she first came from the Azores with the life insurance money from her husband death. She was hoping the account was still active and there was some of the $10,000 left. With the numbers in hand, Doris went to the bank, and a good friend of hers who knew the story started the procedure for a lost passbook. It had to be published in the local newspaper with a thirty-day waiting period before she could close out the account. Those were the longest thirty days of Doris' life.

If Manny saw the ad in the newspaper or went to the bank and tried to clean out the account, her plan would have failed. But Manny, having the passbook in his possession, felt he had nothing to worry about. The day arrived and Doris, with Alicia, returned to the bank where she signed her name and claimed the $2,200 that was left in the account. Manny was left with a useless passbook as a keepsake.

When I remember those days, I think of my mother locking windows and doors while she paced the kitchen waiting for Manny to come and try to get Alicia back. I don't know how she held up. Alicia and her daughter were set up in an apartment just two streets away from our house. She also received custody of her son, five years after she left Manny. She lived in that apartment until her death at the age of 50 as a result of a battle with ovarian cancer. With all the hardship and misery she had to endure in her life she would always smile when Doris entered the room. Alicia's favorite song and the one played at her funeral was, "Your Nobody until Somebody Loves You" by Dean Martin. I know Alicia never doubted her sister Doris loved her and she was always a very special somebody to her.

Money Bags Doris

Doris had a way to take a small sum of money and make it grow. I learned that her secret was to put herself last and her children first. The motto she lived by was, "Give to those who don't have as much as you do or you will never receive anything meaningful out of life in return." Doris was not referring to monetary rewards but emotional satisfaction. Money was never plentiful, but Doris time and friendship was worth millions.

My memories of Doris' physical appearance were that she was always neat and clean. Her wardrobe did not have designer labels; it didn't even come from a department store, off the rack. I would say "Green trash bag" was more appropriate as to how Doris shopped for her clothing. I can remember wondering why her underwear was held up with safety pins, but we always got brand new underwear from the Sears Catalog every September to start school.

I recall getting my first store-bought dress when I was nine years old. It was an apple red jumper with a long sleeve yellow blouse that was covered with little tiny apples. It had a large tie at the neck that formed into a large bow. I felt special wearing such a dress. Up until that time, most of my clothing was hand-me-downs from neighbors that arrived in giant green trash bags. The bags were emptied onto the living room floor and the shopping began. Things were divided into three piles: things that fit now, things that were too big that would be saved for later, and lastly things that were too small that would be passed onto someone else in the neighborhood. Doris was definitely ahead of her time with recycling.

As far as I knew, the bags in the living room were a shopping spree. It wasn't until Junior High when I met my best friend that I realized that most people's idea of a shopping spree were trips into Boston to Filenes and Jordan Marsh for their seasonal wardrobe changes. Even today, I'm known as the clothes broker in my upper middle class neighborhood. Some of my wealthy friends will give me their clothes, some still with tags, to find a good home for them. Today they come in white bags, shoes still in boxes, and designer dresses on hangers, but the concept hasn't changed.

In the 60s and 70s, Doris would never have thought to go to a department store to spend money on new merchandise. The family's money was only there for the essentials: rent, food, and parochial school. Until this one special day when Doris shocked us all with her extravagant purchase.

The Diamond Ring

In her early twenties, Doris worked as a bookkeeper at an exclusive woman's clothing store in Salem, Massachusetts. They catered to the rich and pampered women of Marblehead and Manchester by the Sea. The average cost of a dress was 300 dollars, when the typical person earned $15 a week. Her boss, Mr. B., loved Doris and always managed to have the dress she wanted to fall within her price range. I've seen pictures of Doris in a black cashmere knit dress with hat, purse and coat to match. What a knock out.

Daniel Lowes was another upscale store in Salem that sold sterling silver flatware, china and lots of jewelry, especially diamonds. A store crammed full of all the material things that Doris could care less about, or so I thought.

In the early 70s, my mother's marriage to my father was not doing well. I used to joke that if this was an example of a happy marriage, I would hate to see one on the rocks. Doris decided that if she died, my father wasn't going to get her life insurance money. So she cashed in her policy for $1,100.

Doris got it into her head that a diamond engagement ring would be a nice way to invest the money. This way if and when she died there would be something special, a legacy to give to her only daughter, me. Doris has always had a matter of fact way about talking about "when she goes," but it always made me scared that she knew something I didn't know about her health. But I guess it was just her way, plan for the unexpected and it will not happen.

When I was young I don't recall my father buying my mother any jewelry or any gifts for that matter. The only gift I ever remember he gave her was an electric shaver the previous Christmas. Doris was a little surprised, but she was shocked later that month when she learned that he had charged it to her account. What a guy.

The day after the insurance check arrived, my mother asked me to join her on a shopping trip to Daniel Lowes. Her mission was to pick out the engagement ring she never had. I changed out of my school uniform into my play clothes, which consisted of patched jeans, a striped jersey and my white Keds. Doris had on a three-quarter-length blue plaid coat, light blue claim diggers and old, worn, navy blue boat shoes. I remember feeling a little embarrassed about Doris appearance, and the sudden limp she had developed overnight.

There it was in front of us, this large three-story old red brick building that took up the entire corner of a city block. We walked into the first floor through two large wooden glass doors onto a very creaky old wooden floor. I tried to take it all in at once, but the store was enormous. In the center of the store were porcelain figurines: Hummels, Dresden, and Sebastians. Along the outer walls were cases of beautiful leather goods: purses, briefcases, and gloves. Then I glanced to my left and saw the 'L' shaped glass jewelry case that ran the entire perimeter of the store. All I remember was a sea of lights causing everything in the case to sparkle. Doris had spotted what she was after and in we went.

Doris saw a sales woman at the far end of the case. She was approximately 55 years old, perfectly groomed in her two-piece blue knit suit and had not a single hair out of place. We started walking towards her. We stood there for a few minutes, and the woman turned her back to us as if we didn't exist. Doris politely said, "Excuse me, can you help us?" To which the woman replied, "I'm busy with another customer's order." She proceeded to play with paper work. I felt like "white trash" because Doris was not wearing a fine wool or fur coat, and I wasn't dressed in my "Sunday Best." This woman made me feel worthless. Nothing, not even this woman, would stop Doris from achieving her mission.

What was Doris going to do next? We started walking the other way towards the case of rings. I had never seen so many beautiful diamonds in all different shapes and sizes, glistening under the lights. Suddenly an older gentleman emerged from the back room. From the other woman's attitude, I half expected that this gentleman had already called security. Instead, he looked at my mother with big blue eyes and a kind smile and said, "May I help you ladies?" Doris replied, "Yes, you may. I'm looking for a round cut, diamond solitaire engagement ring as big as $1,100 will get me." He took out a 10×10 inch tray of rings, placed it on a royal blue velvet cloth and began. I don't remember how long it took, but it seemed like only a matter of seconds before Doris had the most beautiful ¾ carat diamond ring on her left ring finger. It was a perfect fit.

The salesman presented Doris with the written bill and asked how she would like to pay for the ring. What happened next shocked me. She took off her left shoe and removed eleven $100 bills wrapped in plastic wrap! Thus the mystery of the sudden limp I had noticed earlier had been solved. Doris didn't believe in pocketbooks due to a rash of muggings in our neighborhood. My mother had used her left-sneaker as a purse to assure the crisp $100 bills would arrive at their destination without incident.

I hadn't thought about this story for a long time until I saw the movie, *Pretty Woman* with Julia Roberts. In one famous scene, she returns to the exclusive boutique that refused to serve her the previous day with all of her new items in hand. She walks up to the sales woman and says, "Do you remember me? I came in here yesterday, and you wouldn't wait on me. You work on commission, right?" The woman replied yes and she then proceeds to say, "Big mistake . . . huge. I have to go shopping now!" Well, Doris may not be Julia Roberts, but they could have written that scene from what happened next.

I couldn't believe it. Doris had bought a diamond ring. I started to head for the exit. To my surprise, Doris was heading in the opposite direction towards her favorite sales woman. Doris stood patiently at the counter while the woman finished with another customer. When she was done, Doris said, "Excuse me. Do you work on commission?" To which the woman replied, "Yes." Doris held out her left hand, placing her ring finger directly under the woman's nose, and said, "Learn. Never judge a book by its cover. You just lost a commission. Have a nice day." I was never more proud of Doris than on that day because she never pretended to be someone or something she wasn't. What you see is what you get, and this time it sparkled.

Bingo

Doris and her mother's side of the family always had this sixth sense. One day, at 2 in the morning, my grandmother Teodolinda came running down the stairs screaming that something terrible was going to happen to me. I had been placed on penicillin a few days prior for strep throat. Within hours of her prediction, I woke up with hives, a swollen face and difficulty breathing. I was having an anaphylactic reaction to the antibiotic. Was it a coincidence?

I recall another incident, involving Doris, when I was thirteen years old. I came downstairs to get ready for school, and there was my mother sitting at the kitchen table. Her face was white as a sheet. I became alarmed and asked her what was wrong. She explained that at 3 A.M. she awoke from a sound sleep after having a very strange dream. She dreamt that a man named George, the love of her life, was saying goodbye and was walking off into the distance toward people she knew in her life that were all deceased. I was young, but I knew that this wasn't an ordinary dream. Within ten minutes, the phone rang and it was my mother's cousin Manny, who had introduced her to George in the early 1940s. He called to tell her that George had been found dead at the bar that he owned. His approximate time of death was 3 A.M. Was it a coincidence?

After many such incidences, I started listening to Doris' premonitions and dreams. When I arrived home from college one afternoon, Doris informed me we were going to play Bingo! This was a little odd considering my mother had very rarely played Bingo, since she preferred playing her numbers with the local bookie. (This was all prior to legal state lotteries, of course.) I was a little confused as to the sudden urge to play Bingo. I tried to bow out, claiming I had too much homework, but Doris was unshakable. So I asked, "Why tonight?" With a straight face, Doris said, "A bird shit on my car, and that's good luck, so we're going!"

Six P.M. rolled around, and we were off to St. James Church Bingo Hall about a mile away. You have to give the Catholics credit: in the 60s and 70s they had cornered legal gambling in the name of God! Unfortunately, in the 70s, people were unaware of the dangers of second-hand smoke. There was no such thing as a non-smoking Bingo hall.

For those of you who have not experienced a night of Bingo, let me try and set the stage. You enter the basement of a very large, old, Gothic-style church that has a damp musty smell. When you first enter the hall, for as far as the eye can see, there are long 3×8 foot tables with metal folding chairs of all sizes and shapes in various states of disarray. The diehard Bingo players are what really get your attention. Little old ladies with blue hair, cigarettes hanging out the side of their mouth and makeup that resembles a painted-on clown face. Their various lucky charms and voodoo magic, like colored rabbit's feet, bobble head dolls of Elvis, huddled in front of them. There was definitely a territorial mentality about who could sit where, and God forbid you went to the wrong table and invaded someone's lucky space.

At the front of the hall was God. Not your normal wooden crucifix with a ceramic Jesus on it, but rather a 2×4 metallic cage that held all the sacred Bingo balls, just waiting for that puff of air that would gently tussle one until it escaped out of the orifice at the top. Next was the all-important man, never a woman, who was trusted with yelling out the bingo numbers. He was usually heavy-set with his abdomen protruding over the top of his belt, instilling fear in everyone if his belt was ever to let go.

Lastly, there were the runners—ironically men too over-weight and out of shape to ever run a day in their life. These were the men who hovered around the perimeter of the hall just wait-ing for someone to call out, "BINGO!" They were trusted with checking the Bingo card of the potential winner by yelling the numbers back to the caller and then issuing the words every player dreamed of hearing: "We have a good Bingo!" The runner also had the pleasure of delivering the winnings, cold cash.

During the 70s, we still used individual cardboard cards and colorful clear tabs to cover and keep track of the called numbers. The typical player would line up three cards down and as many across as they could handle. One wrong cough or sneeze or bump of the table, and the game was history. The tabs would fly every-where. It wasn't until the 80s and the beginning of the disposable game pieces that someone invented throw-away paper sheets and "the dabber." The Dabber was a small four-inch bottle containing various color dyes and a roller ball at the top, which is simply inverted and dabbed onto the disposable card. No fuss, no muss bingo, and no chance of a bingo catastrophe.

Throughout my life, I have been referred to as a double 'A' personality, able to multi-task and do ten things at once, with the exception of multiple Bingo cards. Doris was no better, and nine cards each was our limit. As we sat waiting for the Bingo game to start, we were in awe of the 80 year olds with up to 36 cards in front of them. There was also the famous woman who played eighteen cards and never placed a tab on any of them. Rumor had it that she had a photographic memory or was a savant. I person-ally thought she might be mentally ill, since no one could recall her ever winning a game.

Doris was the most generous person I had ever met and was never greedy, and one of her favorite sayings was, "One bird in the hand is better than two in the bush." At twenty years old, I guess I hadn't quite learned that lesson. Just as the man was about to press the lever to begin game number one—a regular game of Bingo, straight across, diagonal, up and down, or four corners—for fifty dollars, Doris made me a proposition, "I know I'm going to win the coverall for $500. Do you want to make a deal, and split all our winnings down the middle 50/50?" I gave it some thought for a few seconds and replied, "No, thank you." I felt lucky too and didn't want to share. Call me young and foolish, or more accurately greedy and selfish. So the Bingo game was underway.

The fifth game was always the letter 'H', down the 'B', up the 'G' and across the middle using the well-known free space for $100. I knew this was going to be my game; I could smell the $100. I had only two numbers left when he called 'O 72'. I was down to one. I remember concentrating very hard repeating in my mind, "B 5, B 5." I thought I was hearing things when the caller said 'B5', and with a yell that could shatter glass I found myself shouting, "BINGO!" My yell almost deafened the people sitting around us, and Doris came out of her chair not realizing that I was waiting. As I looked up, there was "the runner." He took my card, started the ritual, and said the wonderful words, "We have a good Bingo! Is there anyone else?" I did a split-second scan of the hall, and no hands were raised, no one was moving: I had done it. One hundred dollars was all mine. To put a $100 into perspective, I was paying $400 a semester for state college tuition.

I looked up, and Doris was sitting across form me with a grin on her face. "Congratulations, can I interest you in my proposition again? 50/50" Was she crazy? I was up $100 and she was at zero. "No, thank you. I am happy with my hundred." They were my fatal last words.

A typical Bingo night was twenty games, including five special games, which paid a $100 and a $200 prize for the picture frame.

For the final game, "the coverall," a new set of cards was required, and the first one to cover every number on the card got $500, tax-free. The night progressed on, and suddenly Doris yelled Bingo, winning a $50 game by herself. Once again she asked, "You sure you don't want to split 50/50?" And once again I replied, "No, thank you."

Five minutes later nd Doris once again utttered "Bingo." Was I having an auditory hallucination? She had won the four corners special game, which was worth $100. I looked at her for the previous offer, but it was no longer on the table. "Mom, how about we split 50/50?" I asked. Doris looked up at me from across the table and said, "Sorry, you had your chance. Now play." I felt as though I had passed into another dimension. It wasn't possible for one person to win this many games alone, and the night was only half over. As I scanned the hall, the other players were also in disbelief. They were especially stunned when within ten minutes Doris had called Bingo for the fourth time for the $200 picture frame game. If I hadn't been so greedy, I would have had $225 instead of my lousy $100.

There was a short ten-minute break so everyone could get his or her mojo going for the coverall. There were the rituals of rubbing the lucky rabbit's foot, walking around the table three times counter-clockwise, and the spraying of the holy water. Doris just sat and waited. She didn't go to the bathroom, get anything to eat or drink, or say a word. She just sat and waited. I started to get anxious. I'd never known Doris not to do what she set out to do and those words she'd spoken that afternoon in the front hall came back to haunt me: "We're going to Bingo, and I'm going to win the coverall." No, she couldn't. The crowd was already glaring at her. I felt like the Catholics in the Coliseum in Rome about to be stoned or eaten by the lions at any moment.

Mr. Bingo gave the instructions, "First person to cover the entire card will win $500. Good luck." My only hope was that if she won, it would be split with another Bingo player. Would we get to the parking lot without being mugged? Time was ticking away. I wasn't even paying attention to my own cards because I was too busy watching Doris. She sat emotionless. He called 'B6.' Doris now had two spaces left, N33. It couldn't be happening: she was down to one space. In slow motion, the number O 72 echoed out across the silent hall. "BINGO!!!" Please someone else, anyone, two people. But the hall lay quiet. The same runner came to our table and began the task of calling out the 24 numbers. You could hear a pin drop. No one moved a muscle. Then over the microphone came, "We have a good Bingo for $500."

I think I heard clapping, but I wasn't sure. I suddenly felt bile rising up into my throat, and I kept thinking, "We have to get home." The man returned with Doris' $500 and she proceeded to count out $100 and hand it back to the gentleman saying, "For the church. Thank you." She then divided her winnings, placing half in each shoe. Three of the Bingo men walked us to our car. I think they also feared for our safety. I drove home in a roundabout way, in case someone was following us, but no one did. Everyone around Doris saw her quietly hand back some of the money from her winnings, and they were shocked. After all, Bingo was a way of raising money for the church, wasn't it? Doris' belief was that you always share your good fortune with others

The story wasn't quite over then. I had to promise not to let my brothers know how much she had made that night. She handed each of my brothers $25 and I got zero. I had my $100 after all. How amazing that at 7:30 P.M. I was $100 richer, but by 10:30 P.M. it seemed like a pittance. I went to bed that night wanting to kick myself for not doing the 50/50 split and not believing that when Doris says she's going to win money, she does.

From that day on, whenever my mother and I graced a Bingo hall, we did the 50/50 split. Sometimes I came out ahead, and sometimes I didn't. What I really enjoyed most was spending time with my mother. Okay, maybe getting to scream out Bingo at the top of my lungs didn't hurt either.

You might wonder what Doris did with the remaining $700. One of her best friend's daughters was getting married the following weekend. Elizabeth got a $100 gift instead of $20. A month later, a salesman came to the door selling stainless steel cookware. My mother had known this man from the neighborhood so she purchased a set of cookware at the cost of $350. She bought the pots and pans not for her use; they were to be put aside for my future. I had been accumulating items in my hope chest or as my brothers affectingly called it the "Hopeless Chest." The chest was growing with the vision of marriage some day, if I ever got a date. It was an added benefit that the salesman made a commission to help support his family that week.

One way or another, I did end up getting half of her winnings, not before learning an important lesson. If a bird shits on your car, and you're feeling lucky, buy a lottery ticket or try your hand at bingo. Just remember to split 50/50. You might hit it big. Or you might just need a car wash.

Stock Market

If you asked me today if I would ask Doris for financial advice, the answer would be a definite, "Hell no!" When we were young (before my parents divorced), Doris only worked for short periods of time, for specific purposes: Christmas help for six weeks to get money for our Christmas gifts; summers in a glue factory packing boxes so we'd have money for a real vacation the following year. She had an uncanny ability to take a few dollars and make it multiply. I learned early in my life that you work hard for your money, save as much as you can, and don't take chances with money you can't afford to lose. Another big lesson was that you always put yourself last and go without because your kids and family come first.

Doris finally entered the workforce full time as a bookkeeper in a one-girl office. It was in a leather factory walking distance from our house. Peabody used to be the leather Capitol of the world for tanning and finishing leather. There were still a few factories in business in the early 70s, but the numbers were dwindling due to the invention of less expensive synthetics like naugahide.

We felt that Doris never earned what she was worth from her boss. She had to practically beg for any raises. I could never understand why when he did offer her 5% she would only take 4%. Doris sort of banked it and added the remaining 1% to her next raise the following year. She explained it to me once. Because of the income tax tables, if she took the full 5%, it would bump her into the next highest bracket, and she would pay more state and federal taxes on a weekly basis. Therefore, she would actually bring home less net money each week. Her mentality was not to worry about her gross income, but how much she brought home weekly to run her household.

Doris was very conservative with the little savings she had. She only used a passbook or certificate of deposit because they were insured by the FDIC for $100,000. Once my grandmother decided to part with $1,000 cash and gave it to Doris to do with as she pleased. I think my grandmother had the idea that she might buy herself something frivolous, go out and splurge a little. Instead, a new Doris emerged, a daredevil, who began to dabble into the stock market.

In the early 60s, the average lower-middle class families did not buy stocks. Only the rich and famous, like the Kennedys bought and sold. At the time, a young couple had moved in to the three family house across the street and the husband had just started at an entry-level position at a company called Combined

Insurance of America. Doris felt it was a good place to start. People bought health insurance, and most families were starting to think of life insurance as a good investment. What the hell, Doris thought if Ed worked there it must be a good company. She purchased 100 shares at $2.00 a share.

My father was a sportsaholic. Every weekend he could be found sitting in his Lazy-Boy, with two televisions stacked in front of him and a transistor radio by his side with the earplug in one ear. Considering there were only three stations on television, he had the majority of sporting events covered. All of a sudden, there was the NFL (National Football League) and Massachusetts developed a football franchise named the Boston Patriots. Doris felt there must be other husbands like hers who were obsessed with football, so she purchased 100 shares of Patriots stock at $5.00 a share. The NFL was relatively new and the team's first year was a disaster. The stock plummeted to $0.25 a share. Doris threw the paper shares into a drawer and said, "I haven't lost anything unless I sell them." She then proceeded to forget about them.

Doris would get a hunch or like the name of a company and she would buy the stock. She bought things like AT&T thinking everyone uses a phone at some time in their day. All the neighbors now had their own private lines, no more sharing party lines, so the phone business seemed a safe bet. She bought Proctor and Gamble because everyone needed soap and, of course, toilet paper. Doris' philosophy was to be patient, sell the initial investment when stocks split or went up, and keep the difference. The rule she never broke was "never be greedy."

A few years later, low and behold, the Patriots became the New England Patriots and the NFL was taking off. Back to the sock drawer she went. Her $5.00 a share stock that had gone as low as 25 cents was now selling for $25 a share. Doris broke her own rule and sold them all.

For the one and only time in my life, I can remember my mother went on a buying spree. She purchased a year-old maroon ford station wagon with the rear-facing third seat and eight-track cassette system. Then the 17-foot travel trailer and the beginning of our camping life. Combined Insurance was also doing well and had a two-for-one split. She sold her initial investment and kept the rest. Doris had found a way to make money that didn't involve hard labor. Doris kept this up until the stock market became too volatile, and then she went back to her standby CDs and U.S. Savings Bonds.

While she invested in the stock market for probably six or seven years, she had a loyal following of stock groupies. Her friends would come over and ask her opinion and if she had bought any new stocks that week. I suppose it was a precursor of the first neighborhood stock club. The only difference was that there was no research into the emerging companies or financial statements to review. It was Doris, her sixth sense, and common sense. When I look back, it was a scary way to invest money.

Apparently, I didn't pay enough attention to Doris' method. I recently started to dabble in the stock market, but I didn't listen to her advice. That old greedy monster came out. I was doing very well with a particular stock when it split two-for-one. Doris kept telling me, "Sell and get your initial investment back and keep the rest." Unfortunately, I didn't listen and I nearly lost my shirt. That investment is still located in the bottom of my sock drawer.

Doris The Camper

After Doris' big score on the stock market, she bought a new, 17-foot, Swiss Colony travel trailer. It became our summer home, if you could call it that. It was compact and self-contained and Doris loved it. For the first summer, our family traveled around New England. Afterwards we set it up on a seasonal site in a new trailer park in Wells, Maine, where it stayed until it was sold in 1969.

The floor plan could only be described as compact. The door was dead center and when you walked in, the floor was 3×3 feet of blue linoleum. Immediately to the left was a small three-burner propane gas stove and beyond it a table with two benches. This banquette transformed into my parents' double bed at night. Above the table was a drop-down bunk with barely eighteen inches of head clearance, where I was designated to sleep. To the immediate right was a bank of five-foot tall closets made of blonde wood in a high-gloss finish. Above the storage was a permanent bunk with a set of privacy curtains that pulled across on golden curtain rings. The larger bunk was the shared sleeping quarters of my two brothers. Directly opposite the front and only door was a bathroom-size sink, two-foot counter and a tall closet door. Behind this door, a bathroom, or at least a toilet, should have existed and didn't. Instead, the door just gave an illusion that we actually had indoor plumbing.

My father was not really the outdoor type, unless he was on the golf course. Give him his Lazy-Boy, television and sports, and his life was complete. Doris, on the other hand, was game for anything. She felt we should spend more time as a family, and camping was her inexpensive solution. We joined a camping association called The Forty Niners and began dragging the trailer behind that green Rambler station wagon every weekend. Our neighbors commented that we resembled the *Beverly Hillbillies* because of our bicycles strapped on the car roof, lawn chairs tied to the back of the trailer and the station wagon filled to the brim. We were off.

Killer Lightning

One particular weekend, we stayed at a campground called Eastern Slopes in North Conway, New Hampshire, in the White Mountains. Each campsite had a wooden roof over the picnic table resembling a carport. There was room to place the trailer and awning to the left of the structure. This particular campground bordered a rushing ice-cold river, flowing right off the mountain.

Even though Doris wanted people to think that she loved the rough outdoors, we had electric and water hook-ups so we wouldn't be without the comforts of home. Doris washed her dishes in a square, yellow, Rubbermaid dishpan outside at the end of the picnic table. She washed them, put them all on a rack, and then poured boiling water, that she heated on the stove in the trailer over them. No germs for Doris. The dishes air-dried in the clean, fresh New Hampshire air.

In the afternoon, my father, brothers, and I, along with half the campers in our group, went down to the river to swim. Doris stayed behind with the other mothers to clean up after lunch and do the dishes. All of a sudden, the weather took a turn for the worse. The wonderful sunny sky began to turn overcast and gray, and the once-calm pine trees began swaying to and fro. The air thickened and an odd calmness fell over the site: the proverbial calm before the storm. The sky suddenly opened up, and the rain came down like sheets of glass. Doris could hardly see the trailer across the road, but she could hear her friend's voice, "Doris, quick, come over for a drink until the storm stops." I thank God that Doris liked to drink alcohol more than she hated doing dishes.

Doris ran the fifty feet to her friend's picnic table. She was just picking up her drink when the Earth shook; there was a bright flash across the street and the wooden roof over her picnic table exploded into flames. It had been hit by lighting. A direct hit into the dishpan and the exact spot Doris had been standing only minutes before. The dishes were reduced to a mound of melted melamine, the picnic table was split in half, and the yellow Rubbermaid dishpan was a puddle of molten plastic on the ground. The rain was still pounding the ground and, like nature's fire brigade, started to put out the fire.

My family was unaware at the time what was happening. We were all huddled under the food pavilion roof by the river waiting for the storm to pass. We did know something bad had just happened because the ground beneath our feet had shaken. A few of the parents stayed with the children while the rest of us ran towards the site of the flash and crash. I remember having a terrible feeling that my mother was hurt. I remember silently praying, "Please God, don't let anything have happened to my mother." I could see the same fear in my older brother's face.

We arrived at the site, and low and behold, Doris was safe and sound across the road sipping her drink. I think that week's drink of choice was a coffee sombrero. The local fire department had been called and was on the scene making sure the fire was truly extinguished. When the smoke had finally cleared and the storm had subsided, we went back across the dirt road to assess the damage. All that was salvageable was a deformed, green plastic cup that now had an oval top and a spout where the edge had begun to melt away. Doris estimated that she had only been away from the table for about three minutes before the lightning struck. She kept the green cup as a reminder of what almost happened that day.

The following year, we put the trailer at a permanent site in Wells, Maine, on a seasonal basis. It stayed on C1, a corner lot, with water and electric hook ups, but no sewage for six years. I never asked why they chose Maine. Was it because of the ocean down the street, or the lack of mountains and killer lightning that New Hampshire offered?

Campfires

Doris loved camping and spending her summers with her children in Maine. We walked everywhere, to the beach for ice cream and to the corner store. We only had one car, and my father had it during the week so he could work at home and then drive up on weekends. Sometimes our little jaunts would be five or six miles long, and my poor baby brother Toney would ride on Junior's shoulders when he got tired. The one thing everybody enjoyed the most was the campfires at night. Doris would make herself a cocktail after it got dark and sit in front of the fire staring into the shooting flames. The only problem was getting the firewood. We didn't have a fireplace or any source for firewood at our house in Peabody, and the campground sold a bundle of six pieces for $1.50, which we couldn't afford. It was illegal to cut trees down on private property and we didn't own a wooded lot, so what was Doris to do?

When Dad came up, Doris had the idea to go for a ride inland towards Sanford, Maine, on her quest for firewood. In the early seventies, there was very little development once you went away from the coast, just forest as far as the eye could see. Doris wasn't planning anything illegal like cutting trees down. Her goal was to collect pieces from the side of the road that had just fallen down naturally. It wouldn't be stealing or trespassing; it was more like helping the environment and cleaning up.

We came to an area along a deserted road. There weren't any "No Trespassing" signs posted or inhabitants to be seen, so Dad pulled over. Doris was worried about Toney since he was so small, so he stayed in the car with Dad at the wheel in case a quick get-away was warranted. So Junior, Mom and I started collecting small logs and kindling and loaded up the back of the station wagon. I didn't know one tree from another, but I knew Doris liked the logs with the white bark. I later learned it was Birch, so I scouted the woods for those. It took us only twenty minutes to fill the station wagon to capacity.

When I think back to this time, I wonder if it was worth it. You see, Doris loved the campground, but she wasn't exactly what you would call nature savvy. She didn't know how to identify different plant species or what should be labeled "Do Not Touch." I guess in our haste we hadn't noticed all the red leaves that the free firewood sat in. I wish we had known, because within 48 hours we were all covered from head to toe in Poison Sumac.

It was a poor idea to collect wood in short sleeves, shorts and sandals, because every piece of exposed skin was affected. We had extremely itchy patches all over our bodies that were dark red with small fluid vesicles. Unfortunately for my brother he had needed to relieve himself during our scavenger hunt and now some very sensitive parts of his anatomy were adversely affected by the encounter. At least we had enough firewood for the entire season. Seven nights a week, barring inclement weather, we were out watching the flames dance while we itched ourselves raw. As far as Doris was concerned, it was a small price to pay since we had saved about $200 as compared to the $5 we spent on a few bottles of calamine lotion, "Such a deal!"

The Shower

Beach Acres was a campground that was created out of a large grassy field. Small willow trees had been planted strategically around the grounds that would eventually get large enough to produce shade. It was impeccably kept, and the bathhouses were immaculate.

The bathhouse was a rectangular, cinder-block building that ran approximately 60 feet long by 20 feet wide and was located in the center of the campground. It was accessed from either side by white pine doors labeled "Male" and "Female" leading into identical rooms with ten toilets on the one side, hidden behind wooden enclosures. On the opposite wall were 10 white porcelain wall sinks with a small mirror hanging above each.

At the ends of the building were two showers on each side. The cement dressing area had hooks for clothes and towels on the back of the door. Directly through the white plastic shower curtain was the 4×4 foot shower itself. The floor pitched toward the center with a large silver floor drain waiting to carry dirty water away. Protruding out of the far wall was the showerhead with two hand controls to adjust water temperature. When we started camping, the showers were free. Due to the carelessness of the campers leaving the water running, taking excessively long showers, this privilege was ruined for everyone.

The solution for the campground was to install coin-operated showers with time regulators. You would enter the outer part of the shower, remove your clothing, hang it on the hooks, deposit the money into the slot, turn the timer, and the water would start flowing. The cost was 10 cents for three minutes and 25 cents for nine minutes, which did not sit well with Doris. She had always been very conservative with her water usage, and it was simply another family expense she had to budget for. Doris tried to come up with ways to get the most for her money. She would send my brothers in together to share a shower time and get two clean for the price of one.

Another family expense involving precious water was the laundry. Since we were there all summer without going home and had a limited wardrobe, Doris had to be creative. There was a public Laundromat about a mile away from the campground, and it cost 10 cents for a wash and 25 cents to dry a load. She would only use the Laundromat if we had long spells of rain and general dampness. Otherwise, Doris had a three-foot-tall, pink diaper pail that had been ours as children. Every evening after we would change for bed, she would begin the ritual of doing our dirty laundry in the pink pail. She would fill the bucket with hot water and detergent, and soak the whites overnight. The next morning, she would scrub, rinse and hang them out on a clothesline behind the trailer. The end results were clean clothing with minimal to no monetary expenditure.

Doris has always been a compulsive person, and it is a trait that she has passed on to me. Whenever a thought popped into her head she would often act on it before thinking it through and fully weighing the consequences. She lacked that all important 10 second delay. Sometimes things worked out, but sometimes they didn't. This mentality is what got Doris into trouble in this instance.

We had all returned from a beautiful day at the beach, and it was time for a shower. Junior and Toney would share a three-minute shower, and Doris and I would each get our own luxurious three minutes. I'm not sure, but Junior might have been lucky enough to get a quarter occasionally so he could splurge for the nine minutes, since he did have my younger brother Toney to get squeaky clean.

Doris and I were in opposite showers at the far end of the bathhouse armed with 50 cent flip-flops to guard against the dreaded athlete's foot. I remember putting my dime in the appropriate slot and stripping down to the buff. Soap in hand and shampoo within reach, I turned the lever. Instant water and a quick regulation of temperature, and I was off. Three minutes doesn't seem like a lot, but after doing it for two months, I had the timing down to perfection. Wet entire body, shampoo hair, soap body, and finally rinse thoroughly. If there was still water, just stand and enjoy the hot spray. My shower ended, and I pulled the curtain open to enter the outer area to dry off and dress. The challenge was always to get dressed without dropping your clothes into the puddle that would develop in the center of the floor.

Doris' water was still running after mine had finished, and I was half dressed before her water finally ceased. All of a sudden the four-letter words started flying. "Shit! What an asshole! How could I be so stupid?" I hurried to finish dressing, all the time calling to her, "Mom! What's the matter?" But there was no answer. I unlocked my door, threw my stuff in my bag and ran around the other side of the building to where my mother was. I started knocking on her door, "Mom! Mom! Talk to me!"

Just then the click of the door signaled the lock release, the door opened a crack, and there stood Doris still dripping wet and holding a totally saturated bath towel. I asked, "Mom, what happened? Did you drop your towel on the floor?" I knew from experience that a quick drop to the floor might produce a wet patch, nothing like the level of saturation seen here. The only possibility I could think of was that Doris had intentionally held the towel under the spray. But why would she do that? Doris' explanation was that she suddenly had an idea. She had finished her shower and still had water, so why not wash the towel? The only problem being, that the intended use for a dry bath towel was to dry a wet body prior to saturating the towel under the faucet and rendering it useless. Once again she had one of those potential brilliant ideas that just wasn't quite thought through.

I was able to run to our campsite, sneak her a dry towel and carry the reminder of her memory lapse home without any further embarrassment on her part. I thought the incident was over. I wasn't going to tell anyone, and I figured my mother would want to keep it a secret. Imagine my shock when she personally related the story to everyone she saw that night at the campfire. Doris shared every detail and everyone laughed so hard that one woman came very close to having an accident. I was mortified. How could she let people laugh at her like that? What I realized was that everyone was actually laughing with her. My mother used humor to display her imperfections. By sharing with people, she showed that she was simply human and imperfect. What you see is what you get.

As the years went on, there were times when my mother did or said something and I would feel a quick ping of embarrassment. It would disappear almost instantly because I had nothing to be embarrassed about. She was my mother and was the most sincere person I've ever known. If she wanted to use herself to make people laugh, it was her right. Doris can bring out the best in people. My mother has a unique way of making people see their frailties and quirks as assets, not liabilities.

Politically Incorrect Doris

To say that Doris is priceless, one of a kind, they broke the mold when God created her, is the best way to try and explain "The Phenomena" that is Doris. In her school days, she was an A student in Math and dirty jokes and C or D in everything else. What she lacked in grades she made up in personality.

To this day, as it was when I was growing up, you can't take her anywhere. Whether it is the mall, a restaurant or a school function, she always knows someone and has to talk to everyone. I mean talk, not just "Hi, nice to meet you" or "Have a nice day," but talk. Doris has to discuss such topics as place of birth, number of children and marital status. Doris always has a new joke that she just learned or funny story to relate. It never ceases to amaze me the way people are drawn to Doris and start relating their life stories to her only minutes after they meet.

Over the years, Doris has been compared to Norm Crosby, the comedian known for his unintentional massacre of the English language. She says Shep-Peppers for the soda brand Schweppes, the spice oregano is said ora-gano and my favorite parm-a-zanian for Parmesan cheese are only a few. I have my theories about her problems with spelling and grammar. She grew up in a home where Azorean Portuguese was her first language, and it was more a slang version than proper Portuguese. What could you expect? Her mother, Teodolinda, spoke broken English even after living in this country over 60 years. Her father, Joseph, was the Renaissance man; he could grow anything or brew the best spirits, but he couldn't read or write. He signed his name with an X his entire life. It was not a surprise to me that Doris wasn't given the basics of proper grammar, etiquette, and decorum in public situations. Instead she was just Doris, unique, 100% genuine in every word and action.

Nuns

In the 1960s, the nuns in our parish were very sheltered. The mothers of the students took turns taking the sisters to appointments and food shopping since they didn't have a car. They still wore the long black habits from their heads down to their toes. The outfit started with a black hood covering the head and neck, with a stiff two-inch white band across the forehead that ended just above the eyebrows. Anchored from the hood was a waist-length veil that covered their backs and hid any hint as to how their dresses were fastened. Around the neck and covering the entire chest was a bib that looked like a giant white cardboard flying saucer. The habit was tied at the waist by a large set of wooden Rosary beads, which ended with a three-inch crucifix. The only flesh that was visible to the naked eye was their face below the forehead and their hands. Sometimes even their hands were hidden in secret pockets under the front flap of their dresses.

Doris was one of the volunteer mothers who saw to the needs of the sisters, only her duties went even further. Most people had a healthy fear of the sisters, but Doris feared no one, not even the brides of Christ. Christmas was fast approaching and, once again Doris was in charge of procuring the gifts for her children's three classes. Each child was asked to donate what he or she could afford. Since some of these good Catholic families had as many as 6–13 children, the usual rule was a dollar per child. At a time when there were no restrictions on class size, the church's motto was "As many children as desks can fit into a room." I had 52 children in my class, so this guaranteed my sister a nice gift.

With approximately $150 dollars in hand for 3 gifts, off Doris went to our mall to do a little shopping. Yes, we had a mall. It was built just after I was born in 1958. It had approximately 20 stores, with the anchors being the two giant department stores: Jordan Marsh and Filenes. The stores were configured in an oval shape with the parking lot around the perimeter, at the back of the stores. There were narrow corridors strategically placed from the parking lot to a giant courtyard at the front entrances of the stores. The courtyard was open to the elements, and the mall didn't have a glass atrium built until the late 70's.

Doris had been very secretive about her purchases. When the last day before the Christmas holiday vacation arrived, Doris walked us to school with the three beautiful wrapped packages and cards in hand. She delivered them to the three classrooms: Sister Mary's first grade; Sister Agnes' fifth grade; and Sister Martha's eighth grade. They all thanked her and put the gifts in the corner of their rooms. They wouldn't open them in front of us, and I always wondered if it was because of etiquette or fear of what Mrs. Brown had purchased.

Well, Christmas break ended and it was January 4th and time to return to school. As was the case every morning, we would wait in front of the school for one of the nuns to come out of the convent, open the front door and let us into our classes and out of the cold. But on this day something strange was about to happen. Thefront door of the convent opened and out came all eight of the sisters at once. Oh my God! Who were these imposters? They looked like Sister Mary, Agnes, Martha and Sister Superior, but they had legs.

Habits that had covered every inch of their beings were gone, and in their place were black A-line dresses that were just below their knees, black hose and sensible black pumps. Gone were all the white accessories on their heads and neck. Instead they all wore a smaller version of the Rosary beads as a necklace. I had just gotten over the shock of seeing their legs when I realized they had hair! All that I held to be true, that they were bald, was a falsehood. Did they also wear underwear? There was my fifth-grade teacher Sister Agnes with light brown curls over her forehead and a short little veil barely covering the back of her head. We all couldn't wait for school to end for the day so we could run home and tell our parents about the sisters' surprise. They would never believe us.

When 2:30 arrived, Mom was waiting at the front door of the school to see her friends' reactions to her little gifts. Doris had played a joke on the sisters, but it turned out that the joke was on her. My mother had been under the same assumption as me that nuns didn't have hair, so she had gotten a deal on hot roller sets of 12 and matching brushes and combs. The real gift was a $50 bill in the card. The Sisters in turn wanted to see the look on Doris face, since they were the ones to pull off the joke that day.

The children started to file out of the building when Doris got a look at Sister Superior. It was honestly the only time I can ever remember that my mother was left speechless. She didn't move, she just stared with her mouth ajar. They all had hair, and not just straight hair, it was all curled.

Doris was hurried into the convent since the sisters still had to acquire winter coats to go with the new look. They told Doris that the changes to the habits had to be kept a secret. They had all been worried about their hair. How were they supposed to style their hair? Some of the sisters' hair had not been seen in public for over 30 years. When the three sisters that had Doris' children opened their joke gifts, it was a prayer answered. Curl it! They had taken a good portion of their vacation experimenting with the rollers and hairstyles, so when the unveiling came on January fourth, they were all ready, thanks to Mrs. Brown.

Some of the mothers felt that the curlers had been in bad taste and not appropriate for a Christmas gift. Doris was stripped of her gift shopping duties the following year. The special Thank You letter that each sister wrote made up for any regrets that Doris might have felt about her choice of gifts. The $50 cash gift actually came in handy in purchasing their new winter coats. My mother knew that she had saved the day with her big joke gift, even if the joke had actually been on her.

Negroes

Doris was born in 1924, so she grew up in during the Great Depression and World War II. She described her neighborhood at that time as poor, filled with one-two- and three-family, owner-occupied houses. It was a diverse group made up of Swedes, Greeks, Portuguese and the Negro family next door. Most people had some type of vegetable garden on their property, fruit trees and livestock, since there was no such thing as a supermarket. They still had horse-drawn carts that came by selling fresh fish, bread and ice for the iceboxes.

When she would tell me stories about the Negroes, I didn't even know what it meant. I knew I was Portuguese and Irish, so

I thought it was another nationality. It wasn't until I was filling out an application for my first job and it asked race that I knew I was called Caucasian for white, and Negro for black. To Doris it only signified a word and description of her neighbors who lived on the right.

Later in life when my brothers and I tried to get her to be more politically correct, it was futile. We introduced her to Black and African American as alternatives to Negro, but we had no luck. Doris would say "When the United Negro College Fund starts calling themselves, The United Black or African American College Fund, I will stop using the word Negro."

Instead of calling people that were born with mental and developmental delays "retards" or "retarded," we asked her to say mentally challenged or mentally delayed. It wasn't going to happen. To Doris, these were only words and depending on what decade you grew up in and when you went to high school, they were constantly changing. One man's politically correct today was another man's politically incorrect tomorrow. We learned an important lesson every day, and that was that her actions always spoke louder than her words.

The Miller family had seven children, five boys and two girls, and lived next to Doris until the late 1930s when she was around 13 years old. Since my mother was the ultimate tomboy, she only played with the boys. She told me about how their grandfather had been a slave down south and fought during the Civil War. When he was freed, he came north and settled in Peabody, Massachusetts. He sat in an old rocking chair on the front porch and smoked a homemade corncob pipe and sang. He died sometime in the 1930s. Doris wasn't sure which year, but she remembered that he was 101 years old and the skin on his face was wrinkled and sagged.

Doris was pregnant with me in the hottest September in 30 years. All she did was sit on the front porch and drink lemonade to try to keep cool. Having had a miscarriage after adopting my older brother, I was technically her first pregnancy and she wasn't doing anything to lose this baby. She noticed a big Buick sedan coming up her quiet street, slow down in front of her house and then drive away. She had also noticed that the passengers were two men, one woman and three children, and yes, they were black.

Suddenly, the car was back and this time it stopped right in front of her house. The driver put the car into park and jumped out. He was heading straight for Doris. I have seen pictures of my mother just before she delivered me and she was huge. She wasn't moving. This 6-foot, 2 inch black man lifted her out of the chair, put her in a bear hug, and said, "Is it really you, Doris? I would know you anywhere. It's me, Michael Miller." It was one of her Negro neighbors, the boy she used to climb trees with, her former partner in crime. He was a Rhode Island State Trooper and was here in Peabody for a funeral. He had to show his wife and children the best place he had ever lived. The shock to find that his best friend Doris still lived next door was nothing short of a miracle.

Michael and his family sat on the porch, while he and Doris reminisced. They talked about climbing trees and the trouble she got him into. His family had lived in many cities since leaving Peabody: Harlem, New York; Roxbury, Massachusetts; and finally in Providence, Rhode Island, where he lived with his family. His brothers and sisters were all over the country and doing well. Before he left, Doris had to take him into his yard so he could see that the apple and cherry trees that they used to climb together were still there.

One of the Miller sons' still lived in Peabody. When I was 10 years old, Doris and I were walking downtown to pay some bills when this black couple came toward us. The man was a little older than Doris, but when he saw her you could see the recognition on his face and she hadn't even uttered a word.

"Doris, is that you? It's me Kevin Miller." Immediately they were in an embrace and they were both smiling. He introduced us to his wife, and she had apparently heard about the famous Doris because she was so genuinely happy to finally meet her.

I was standing on the sidewalk taking it all in when Mom realized I was still there. More introductions and hugs and it was time to say our goodbyes. On the way home, I asked her how she knew these black people. At the time, I had never met a black person. Our neighborhood was white lower-middle class and there were no blacks at my parochial grammar school. I'm talking 1967 and the first black sitcom *Julia* hadn't even been on TV yet. Doris relayed that he was one of the Negro kids that she had grown up with. I thought it was kind of neat that my mother knew a black person.

Ten years passed, and once again Mom and I were walking downtown to Peabody Square when we bumped into Mr. and Mrs. Miller. This time, Kevin looked very thin and frail and had a piece of cloth tied around his neck hiding a tracheotomy. He was not able to talk, and his wife told us he had been operated on for throat cancer. He needed a device to talk and he had left it at home, so she did all the talking. Mrs. Miller invited us to their home that weekend. Doris accepted and, since my mother cures the world with food, asked Kevin what he wanted her to cook. He wrote Kale Soup, a Portuguese favorite.

On Saturday afternoon, Doris called the number she had been given to let them know we were on our way. They lived down a one way street right off of Peabody Square. Their modest house was set in the back behind the other houses at the end of a long narrow driveway, but Doris and I were able to find it without too much trouble. When I knocked at the already opened inner door, this much taller and younger black man answered. Doris was behind me holding the large pot of Kale soup with beans and potatoes, and one large loaf of Portuguese crusty white bread for dunking. She had also decided Kevin could use some of her mother's whiskey buns, which resembled human dog biscuits, so I carried a bag full of them. They were great if you were experiencing a little nausea; one dunk into a cup of tea and it would help to settle the stomach. Also the dough was made with flour, eggs, sugar and one tablespoon of whiskey to give Kevin some added calories that he looked like he needed.

Once we were both into the front hall, it was like a reunion. The front room was full of Kevin's siblings. Word had spread that Doris was coming, and Millers had arrived from three states to see if she had changed any in 40 years. Apparently, the very tall man that had let me in was his younger brother, Michael. Doris informed him that I was the baby she was carrying the last time they had met and made a formal introduction.

Everyone had a Doris story that was more outrageous than the last. It was apparent that my mother was a wild child. I wonder if she had been a kid in my neighborhood when I was growing up if I would have been afraid of her or her friend. I have always been what one might call a goody-two-shoes, afraid I would get caught if I did something bad and I didn't want to encounter the wrath of Doris.

My mother kept in contact with Kevin and his wife and would visit occasionally with a pan of soup or her famous Portuguese Sweet Bread. He survived the throat cancer and died 15 years later from a second cancer. She told me about going to his wake and seeing the Negro family that she had grown up who lived on the right side of her house.

Gays

When I was growing up, I led a very sheltered life: Catholic schools for 12 long years and a very stable home life. I lived in my mother's house until I moved to my current address when I got married at age 25. Among the families I grew up with, most of the parents that are not deceased, are still living in the family homesteads. Even some of the kids I played with have moved back to raise their children on our Street.

I was never exposed to the fact that there were lifestyles other than heterosexual. I didn't really know what heterosexual meant. I knew what I was taught. There was a man and woman, you grow up, get married and have children, in that order. So simple, yet was it really that cut and dry?

Then television had only started to have its impact on American life. There were only two or three stations when I was young, and there were only a few shows to watch. *Leave it To Beaver, The Donna Reed Show* and *The Ed Sullivan Show* made up my world and a glimpse of reality each week. We watched in black and white because my family didn't get our first color TV until 1972 when I was 15 years old. Everyone on TV was always just like me, white, went to school everyday, had a family with a mother and father, and went to church. There wasn't even a show that had a black person. One of my first memories of a black actor on TV was Sammy Davis Jr.

Having the name Leslie didn't leave many options for nick-names. I have my older brother Junior to thank for that since he was the one who named me. My mother gave him three choices for his new baby sister, Elizabeth, Mary or Leslie and we all know what he chose. So that left me with Lez, never Les because that was more the male counterpart. Junior had picked the only name that could be male or female and he chose the male spelling. I don't blame him because he couldn't really read yet, so I lay all the blame on Doris.

When I was 13, a girl at school said I was a Lezzy. I knew it was not a compliment. This particular girl, Kathy, had tormented me for years. She loved to do fat jokes, and one day in the seventh grade, she told everyone I was pregnant. I knew that there was no way that I could have been pregnant unless God performed another immaculate conception. I had no clue what Lezzy meant, so I went home to ask Doris if I was a Lezzy. When I look back at it now, I think my mother was as clueless as I was back then.

Doris could talk about anything but sex. When I finally had learned about the birds and the bees from my cousins, I tried to get verification of a few facts without any luck. When I asked her what a Lezzy was, she seemed a little more nervous than normal. I immediately realized that it must have something to do with sex. My mother did her best to explain that a Lezzy was another word for lesbian. Doris prescribed to the sex education principal of; Answer the question honestly, use words that are age-appropriate to the child, and don't volunteer any more information than is necessary. That is exactly what she did.

I'm not sure how long I sat there trying to figure out what Lesbian meant. I was getting no closer to finding out if I was one. So I tried again and said, "Mom, what is a Lesbian? I don't know what that means." I'm not sure how long I waited for the definition, but I was getting very close to calling my cousin Lucy for the answer. Then Doris did her best to explain something she didn't quite understand herself.

My poor mother started to say there are people who like other people of the same sex, and they are fags and dykes. Once again using the slang terms she was familiar with having growing up in the 1940s. I was no closer to the answer and now had more questions. What is a fag? What is a dyke? I thought a dyke was a wall that held back the water in Holland. What did that have to do with sex? A fag is a man that is feminine and likes other men. What did a man have to do with it? I didn't think Kathy was calling me a guy. A dyke is a woman that likes other women and is masculine. Finally, she tried to explain again. It's when two people of the same sex, two girls or two boys, are together as a couple. OK, we had two people who wanted to date each other; what was so wrong with that? I knew she was leaving something out because she paced around the kitchen and was profusely sweating the more questions I asked. "Can two people of the same sex get married?" I asked. Doris lost it and started yelling. "No, no, no, two people of the same sex can't get married. It has to be a man and woman, so they can have kids."

"What you are saying is that two people of the same sex date and are a couple, but they can never get married, so they can't have sex or children?" I asked. I was still under the impression at 13 years old that you couldn't ever have sex until you were married to that person first. What happened next was as confusing to me as it was for poor Doris. "The church and people think that liking the same sex is wrong. The church says it is a sin. These people, they call them gay, are not allowed to be together legally or go to church. They have to hide their feelings or they can be arrested." Then she looked at me and said, "I know that they do have sex. I just don't understand how." She finally came out and said, "A lesbian is a woman who loves another woman."

I looked at her, and there must have been a look coming over my face because I said, "You mean like Mary and Donna who live across the street? They are always together, they live in the same house, and they seem like they really like each other." Doris smiled and said, "Yes, like Mary and Donna."

The funny part was I didn't think of Kathy's insult as a bad thing if it meant I was like our neighbors. These two wonderful, loving women lived together at a time when it was not acceptable. They shared a two-family home and always had the second floor apartment furnished to keep up the pretense. In those days, they were called two old maids who shared a house. They shared a house and their lives together for over 50 years before they died.

My brothers and I would go over to their house and help them with shoveling or yard work and they would have us into the kitchen for cake and hot cocoa. My baby brother was Donna's favorite of all the neighborhood kids. They were part of our lives: birthdays, graduations and our weddings.

When I think of today and my children, they have grown up with so much more freedom. My husband and I have gay and lesbian friends, and I never tried to hide their lifestyle from my girls. My daughter asked me once why Uncle Paul and Uncle Michael fight, and I told her because they are married. I used my mother's method: only enough information to answer the question. She accepted it and never asked about them again.

Since I am a married mother of two girls and a Nurse Practitioner, I felt that I was now qualified and the time had come to enlighten my mother. Doris finally now knows how same sex couples have sex. She is much more open-minded as she ages.

Doris The Patient

I am happy to report that Doris has always been very healthy for her 80 plus years. Some of that might have to do with good genes. Both of her parents lived to eighty something and her grandparents 90s. One of her grandmothers achieved 100 years and three months.

As a child, I can remember a picture of a very old woman in black with a shawl over her shoulders sitting in front of a cake with a large number 100 on top. It was my Vovo's (grandfather in Portuguese) mother, and he had not seen her since his visit in 1932. I don't recall him ever calling her since neither he nor his mother had a phone. Writing was out of the question since he was illiterate. He would get news when relatives and friends came back from visiting Gracosia. On rare occasions they might bring a letter written by a relative or a picture like this one of his mother's 100th birthday celebration. Joseph died in 1970 when I was 13 years old. My mother had a very special bond with her father and loved him very much. I could see that she was always daddy's little girl even at 46 years old.

The Bug Bite

The only times I remember Doris being ill were two surgeries. There was her gallbladder removal and the legendary hemorrhoidectomy. Once when the family was vacationing in Montreal, Canada she developed blood poison from an infected insect bite. We had taken one of our famous two-week vacations to Quebec and continued to Montreal and the site of the 1967 Worlds Fair. The fact that it was 1970 meant that it wouldn't be as crowded or expensive. Or at least that was Doris logic, better late than never.

The family had become experts on setting up the tent, which wasn't easy since it had rained the past three days. Due to the continued dampness and stagnant water the mosquitoes were vicious. Doris was prepared for all types of mosquitoes with her handy can of repellant, but her mistake was that these bugs were deer flies, not our Maine variety mosquitoes. I swear they were drawn to it, not repelled by the pine sent. No problem, Doris also had the after-bite solution, a concoction she mixed of equal parts boric acid solution, rubbing alcohol and calamine lotion. Once a person was bitten, this potion was applied directly to the bite and the itch and welts were history, or so she thought.

Wednesday morning arrived, and it was the day we had all waited for, the Worlds Fair. All Doris' promises were accurate: there were pavilions, amusement rides and great food, even if it was only half the size of the original fair. But there was a glitch, Doris came out of the tent and she was limping. Sometime in the past 24 hours, my mother had been bitten by something and now her right leg was swollen twice the normal size from her toes to her knee. The entire leg was fire red, hot to the touch and apparently too painful to walk on. Sometimes Doris went too far with the martyr route, and she was determined that she wasn't going to let a bug bite ruin our day. When we arrived at the fairgrounds, she found a bench in the shade and elevated her leg and was going to tough it out for 6–8 hours until we had seen the entire fair.

I can remember being very scared that when we came back at the end of the day, something bad was going to have happened to my mother. We didn't realize at the time that not only was she having a severe allergic reaction to the bite, but also the leg was infected and she had blood poison. Thankfully, when we stopped to have lunch and check on Doris, my mother had come to her senses and knew she was in trouble. We asked security and they directed us to the nearest hospital so Doris could get the medical attention she needed and not a minute too soon.

We arrived at the Emergency Room and Doris hobbled in. They immediately put her in a wheel chair and off to an exam room. Doris was surprised to be treated by a female physician. I wouldn't say she was prejudiced, only all the time I was growing up she encouraged me to be a nurse, not a doctor. I think that was because of the time and the women's equal rights movement wasn't in swing yet. My mother was still under the belief that certain professions were for women and others were for men, and that was the way it was. As the years went on, she would say things that had the women lib tones, such as you never need a man in your life to be complete, you should choose to have a man in your life. She let us follow our own path. Being a wife and mother was a decision we needed to make, not the world around us telling us what to do.

Finally, the doctor wheeled my mother out from the exam room, and with a very thick French accent, she said to Doris, "Now you take medicine with the yogurt and don't let any more bugs bite you or it could be very bad." Doris looked back over her shoulder at the doctor with a quizzical look on her face and I could see it coming. Doris' reply was, "I will be sure to talk to the deer flies and ask them if they could not bite me anymore. Oh, since we are in Montreal, should I ask in English or in French?" The poor woman didn't get Doris' sarcasm. Since we had been coated in repellant, wearing long sleeve everything, and stayed in after dark, what more could we do but talk to the bugs since the other precautions were not helping.

We returned to the campsite, and Doris started the antibiotic with yogurt and hot compress treatments for the blood poison in her leg. I stayed with my mother at the campground the following day to continue the moist compresses, leg elevation, and it began to improve within 24 hours. Doris continued her dialogue with all the nearby deer flies threatening their demise if they dared to take a piece of her flesh. Apparently even in Canada they were afraid of the wrath of Doris.

Hemorrhoids

When I was 10 years old, I can remember Doris having a problem with her bowels. In the 60s, you did not discuss constipation in mixed company. There were no commercials on TV for Exlax or Milk of Magnesia. Only cigarettes, bread and soap powder were openly advertised. I vaguely remember a giant bottle of mineral oil on the counter in the kitchen and what occurred when I had the misfortune of saying that I hadn't moved my bowels in two days. I was given a hefty dose of this W30 weight liquid with a juice chaser and within 24 hours, results. Here was Doris drinking enough of the stuff that she was creating oil slicks on the kitchen chairs from the oil leaking out of her pores.

The problem had surpassed my comprehension and the mineral oil treatment, so Doris went to see the specialist. His name was Dr. Parker, and he was affectionately referred to as Rear Admiral Parker since he was originally a naval physician and specialized in rear end problems. Upon discharge from the Navy, he opened a small practice combination hospital on a beautiful street lined with mansions a block from the ocean. Once again, I began to fear something bad was going to happen to my mother, that she was sick and she might die. I would be left alone with Teodolinda and my father. The thought of the two of them raising me caused such fear and anxiety that I was determined to find out what was wrong.

As a child I was curious, always with a healthy dose of fear thrown in. That afternoon when she returned from the Doctor's office, she was carrying a small blue box approximately 6×6 inches and went directly to her bedroom. Doris was only there a few minutes when she reemerged and everything was back to normal. I had to find out what was in the blue box and I knew Doris wasn't going to volunteer the information.

I made the decision to find the box. I waited until she went to the basement to do the laundry, and in I went. The bedroom was in the back of the house and the shades were all pulled down, so it was dark with eerie shadows on the walls. The dark pine bureau was to the left and the four-poster bed was on the right surrounded by built-in knotty pine cabinets and two closets. My mother loved wood and she included it into every room that she could. It also gave us a lot of extra needed storage in a small four-room apartment that housed five people.

The top of the dresser had handmade crocheted doilies neatly placed in the center and a small, pink rose-flowered lamp to the far end. As I expected, the box was not in plain view. I didn't have much time and I needed to open the drawers. Slowly, I started with the three small drawers on the left. The top drawer was all junk, costume jewelry, scarves, and no box. The second one was filled with nice lingerie. This took me back since Doris always wore old flannel P.J.s and most of her underpants were held up with safety pins. What was she doing with these forbidden under-garments? The jackpot was behind drawer number three. The blue box was just sitting there, and I carefully lifted it out and placed it on the doilie in the center of the bureau.

I was staring at the box for what felt like hours when I had the courage to lift the lid. To my astonishment sat five white plas-tic rocket ships in five different sizes. What where they? I couldn't grasp what little plastic tubes had to do with constipa-tion. I had seen suppositories before when my brother had high fevers and he was given Tylenol, but this was bizarre.

My confusion was to come to an abrupt end when I looked up into the large oval mirror hanging over the dresser and saw Doris standing behind me. Doris had this smirk on her face and she said, "So you found my rectum expanders?" I replied "You're what?" I felt as though she was speaking another language. I knew bum, hinny and ass, but rectum? What or where was that located? My mother to this day can read my face, and knows me better than anyone else, so she could sense my dilemma. Without any hesitation, she explained her problem in layman's terms that a ten-year-old could grasp. It was simple; her ass was too small. Because of this problem, coupled with occasional constipation, she had developed the dreaded hemorrhoids.

The Rear Admiral had developed special rocket shaped, rectal expanders, probably influenced by his military service, to help people avoid hemorrhoid surgery. It was a five-week program of specific exercises, three times a day, starting with small rocket number 1 thru the largest number 5. The premise was you start as a little asshole and 5 weeks later you have become a big ass-hole. I sometimes picture Rear Admiral Parker and the infomer-cial he could have developed in 2009. "Just $19.95 gets your complete set of the five rectal expanders, not two, not three, but five, count them five and prevent those unmentionable problems with hemorrhoids. We'll throw in a free tube of water-soluble lubricant and Preparation H to cool down your backside while you are going through the program. This is a television offer only; they are not available at any store, so call now. Don't miss out on this unbelievable price of $19.95 and $3.95 for shipping and handling." Unfortunately, the treatment failed miserably, even though Doris followed the instructions. She went back to see Dr. Parker.

The day arrived for Doris' surgery, a hemorrhoidectomy, and my father and I drove her to the white mansion near the ocean. I was a little concerned since I had heard the rhymes about Lynn, "Lynn, Lynn, the city of sin. You never come out the way you go in." In Doris' case it was going to be a reality. The doctor had his operating rooms and a little three-bed hospital set up in this 15-room palace, and it was dedicated to rectal procedures only.

I had never seen houses like these. They were all three stories tall, had expansive center staircases that led to elaborate verandas. The entry doors were oversized with stain-glass side panels. A woman in a white dress and cap answered the door and led us into an expansive foyer. In the center was a massive, round cherry table, with ball and claw feet. Centered on the table was a crystal vase overflowing with fresh cut flowers. The marble floor in grey tones, led the way to the "Gone With the Wind" staircase that went up the center of the hall and curved to the left and right. This was unlike any other hospital I had ever seen. No cold tile floors, florescent lighting, sterile white walls or antiseptic smell, instead stained glass, antiques and the smell of lilies.

Now, having been in the health-care field for almost 30 years, the entire enterprise was unbelievable. Here was a single physician running a private hospital and all his services were covered by insurance. The accommodations were like those of a five star hotel and you didn't have to be wealthy to get the care. Today, with HMOs and prior authorizations, Doris probably would have had to wait months for the procedure and have documentation from more than one physician that it was necessary.

Doris was scheduled for the procedure the next morning, five days of recovery, and if all went well, home, as good as new. I wondered if Dr. Parker had a thing for the number five since it seemed to be a common denominator throughout his practice and treatments. My father and I drove to see my mother the next evening and I was afraid she wouldn't look the same or would have tubes in her arm, but she looked beautiful. There she was all propped up on overstuffed feather pillows and wearing this pale peach satin bed jacket with a lace collar and a satin bow at the neckline. All my concerns were replaced with the question, "Where did you get the new pajamas?" Doris explained that they were her special hospital nighties and she kept them in her hope chest. They were only to be used for special occasions. I just equated it with me having new underwear to start school every September, or to wear when going to the doctor.

As my parents were talking, I decided to look around and check out the bathroom. It was enormous, as big as my bedroom, and it had this thing, which I learned later in life was a bidet. Then there was the toilet. The seat was cushioned, no hard wooden seat here, and there were these little hoses that protruded from the back of the bowl. I didn't want to disturb my mother and father's quality time, and I had to go anyway, so why not try it out for myself? Ok, I was done but where was the T.P? There was no toilet paper anywhere. Then I saw this little plaque on the wall with 2 buttons on it. I pressed number one. Oh my God, I almost leapt off the bowl. There was a sudden spray of warm water washing off my hinny. It actually felt good. Button number 2, and I was being blown dry by this warm air. The whole procedure was hands off.

As I departed the bathroom from heaven, I could not get the smile off my face. When I reentered Doris' room, she had sensed that I had test driven her toilet. All she said was, "Have a nice ride?" I now understood why Dr. Parker was so popular, and why there was a six-month waiting period to get in.

The next day, Doris was progressing well when Dr. Parker made his morning rounds. He made it a habit of giving his patients instructions on how to do exercises to tighten their rectal tone after the procedure. They were to tighten and release and tighten and release for sets of 20, 10 times throughout the day. Doris had always been a visual learner. Show her something, and she could copy or follow it without a problem. Dr. Parker also believed in visual cues, so he clenched his fist and released a few times to get his point across. Well somewhere between the verbal instruction and physical demonstration, Doris' brain had a short circuit.

Day four and Dr. Parker was back for his rounds and asked my mother "How are the exercises going?" To which she replied, "Great, but my hands are cramping up a little." I wish I could have been there to see the look on this doctor's face. He looked at her in disbelief, speechless. Doris was his first patient to actually do thousands of tightening and releasing of her hands and not her rectum. To Doris' defense, how was she supposed to know the hand was a visual aid and not to be taken literally? The doctor did have a good point when he reminded her that the surgery had not taken place on her hand. I'm not sure why Doris was released on the spot on day four, breaking Dr. Parker's numerical fixation on the number five, only she was. I understand that he had standards and a reputation to uphold and my mother was definitely putting his livelihood in jeopardy. I don't recall how long the Rear Admiral was in business, but I can guarantee he never had another patient like Doris.

Gallbladder Attack

From as far back as I can remember, I never recall Doris complaining of being in pain. There were times, in Montreal when her leg was swollen and infected, that she had to have pain, but never any complaints. There were the severe migraine headaches that plagued her all her adult life and she never complained. Back in the early 70's there were no special migraine medicines. The treatment consisted of aspirin, a dark quiet room, and your head packed in ice. Doris always seemed to be invincible, a super mom before the phrase was in vogue.

Doris' treatment for most illness, such as upper respiratory infection or body aches was a version of a hot toddy. She would take a two ounce shot of her father's homemade bang bang, 180-proof spirits and set it on fire. A normal saucer from her everyday dishes was placed on the Formica countertop, and the alcohol was carefully poured onto it, assuring no drips. Then a teaspoon of sugar was gently stirred in, as Doris took a regular wooden match and would hold it to the very edge of the plate until the mixture ignited, giving her a pretty blue-pink flame. A few minutes of careful stirring to get all the sugar dissolved and achieve the correct temperature, blow out the flame, and drink slowly.

The effect of this potion was usually 12 hours of deep almost comatose sleep and profuse sweating. Hopefully, the next morning you were cured of what ailed you. I equate it with today's NyQuil or the hot flu over-the-counter remedies, which also include good old ethanol. I had witnessed this ritual more times than I could count until one evening when my mother must have been tired from being up the previous two nights coughing, and things did not go well.

The flaming mixture was glowing on the counter and she was just about to blow it out when the effect of her taking a deep breath caused her to let out a powerful cough. It was not the usual gentle puff of air. No, this was like a sudden gale, and the blue liquid was airborne. It went across the white Formica counter, down the side of her refinished pine cabinets and across the blue linoleum floor. Doris, Mrs. Can Handle Any Situation or Crisis was yelling, "Help! Fire!"

In the late 60s, people were not really trained in fire safety or fire suppression. The movement to have fire drills with your family and the use of fire detectors, which weren't even invented yet, or a fire extinguisher in every kitchen were things yet to come. So, in came my dad, and between the two of them blowing and stomping on the flames there was minimal damage to the kitchen. I don't recall, after that incident, Doris using the hot toddy cure that often.

One morning, many years later I came downstairs to go to school and found Doris sitting at the kitchen table and she didn't look well. Mom wasn't a morning person, but she told me she wasn't going to work because she had been up all night with food poisoning. I didn't buy that story because we had all eaten the hotdogs and potato salad the previous night, and no one else had any symptoms. I went to school and all day had that feeling something bad was going to happen to my mother. I couldn't wait to get home to check on her because there were no cell phones to call her and pay phones in a parochial high school didn't exist.

I ran down the hill to our house, and into the kitchen and called out "MOM!" There was no answer. It was a four-room apartment, so where could she be but the bedroom? There was Doris curled up in a fetal position and rolling from side to side on the bed. Her color was pasty and she was diaphoretic. Oh my God, was she having a heart attack? I was only one year away from starting nursing school, so I had a little medical knowledge and my instincts were to call an ambulance. Doris was able to speak in between the pains and said, "Drive me to the emergency room, now!"

I helped my mother to the car and laid her across the back seat and got in the driver's seat. I thought a little prayer might be in order, so I started to pray silently that she wouldn't die and don't let me have a car accident on the way. I drove fast, but safely as I constantly checked my rear view mirror to make sure Doris was alive. I could hear her let out these moans and when she could speak she would assure me she was fine. Then this loud belch echoed off the windows of the car, and sounded like a belching contest for the title of world's longest, loudest burp. Then there was nothing, silence, and Doris sat up looked at me through the rear view mirror and said, "Let's go home."

To say that I was a little shaken was an understatement. I found a place to pull over and put the car into park. I slowly turned around to face Doris and said, "Go home, are you crazy? One minute you were dying and after one lousy burp you're cured? You want me to believe it was GAS? The past 24 hours of moaning, rolling around the bed and pain, and it was gas? No, I don't buy it." We sat there for a few more minutes and I couldn't get her to change her mind about the ER. We did reach a compromise. She promised to see her general practitioner, Dr. Fowler, the next day, so I drove us home.

Three days later without any of her symptoms ever retuning, I drove my mother to see her doctor. Dr. Fowler was an old-fashioned general practitioner, osteopath, who practiced from a small annex at the back of his home. The white center-entry colonial sat on a corner lot, emerald green shutters hung at every window, and the property was perfectly landscaped. Next to the door at the separate entrance to his office was a small unpretentious sign, that simply read in block letters "Dr. Fowler M.D."

Doris led the way into his little waiting room. It was sparsely decorated with four wooden Hitchcock chairs placed around the perimeter walls, each with a handmade braided chair pad. I hadn't realized a little bell had jiggled when we opened the door to alert the receptionist, alias Mrs. Fowler, that a patient had arrived. The inner door opened immediately and a plump woman appeared. She was in a handsome brown tweed skirt, starched white blouse and low-heeled leather pumps. Mrs. Fowler knew Doris from previous visits and called her by her first name and informed us that the doctor would be out momentarily.

True to her word, within five minutes the door opened and out into the waiting room came the doctor. He was a distinguished man over 6 feet tall with silver-gray hair and he wore a three-quarter length starched white medical coat with his name embroidered over his left breast pocket. Since we had never met, introductions were made and Doris followed him through the mysterious door to an exam room.

It felt as though my mother had been in the exam room for hours and my mind kept racing. Please don't say that it's her heart or cancer. My mother was too young and healthy to die. Out they came and the announcement was made: gallbladder. What a relief, but what was a gallbladder? Should I be happy? Was that a good thing? When I think back and review my career as a nurse practitioner, I realize what a skilled diagnostician this doctor was. He had taken a thorough history of her symptoms and, after her examination, he had made his preliminary diagnosis. He had ordered some lab tests and a gallbladder x-ray to confirm his finding, and he had already booked her in with a surgeon for a consult.

The test results were in and Doris had choleliathiasis, gallstones. Her symptoms had disappeared quickly because the belch released the trapped air and once it dissipated, the stone moved and she had no more pain. Doris was given instructions to have no fat in her diet until the surgery. Fat is what causes the gallbladder to become activated and try to excrete bile that digests the fat, which in turn can cause an attack and severe pain when stones are involved. Mom was booked for her surgery called a choleycystectomy or in layman's terms, gallbladder removal.

In the 1970s, gallbladder surgery was considered a major abdominal procedure. You would be admitted to the hospital the day before for laboratory tests, chest x-ray, EKG, along with the pre-op physical with the anesethiologist. It involved a six-seven inch abdominal incision line transversely across the right upper abdomen just below the rib cage. The size of the incision was proportional to the size of the surgeon's hands. Always keep this concept in mind when choosing your surgeon. Doris was very fortunate that her doctor had very small but extremely skilled hands. The surgery was followed by a week-long hospital stay and six weeks of recuperation at home.

Doris had her surgery without any complications. That evening, we visited and found she wasn't in her room. I had that sudden fear that something bad had happened to my mother, and then we heard that unmistakable voice. Two rooms down the hall, we found her sitting across from an elderly gentleman playing cribbage. She tried to tell us that they had postponed her surgery but she forgot about the I.V. that was hanging above her head. My mother had always said, "Everything in life is mind over matter. You can accomplish anything you set your mind to do and pain is only what your mind tells you it is." So Doris had apparently told herself there was no pain and she believed it.

Unfortunately for the Browns, gallbladder disease ran in both sides of our family. My father had his removed two years later, but he was far from the model patient. In 1991 at the ripe age of thirty three, I had the privilege to be the first laparoscopic cholecystectomy performed by my surgeon and friend. I spent my one night in the hospital per my HMO, one injection of Demerol the night of surgery for pain, and then home on Tylenol. I was back to work as a visiting nurse in nine days. Thank God another thing I inherited from my mother was her mind over matter philosophy.

Doris the Artist

To describe Doris as an artist might be a little bit of a stretch. It might be more appropriate to say she was artistic. Whatever project she got involved in, she always gave it 100% even if the outcome was far from perfection. My mother's life when I was growing up revolved around her three children and their lives. Then one day she read in the newspaper about adult evening classes that were about to begin at Peabody High School. It was perfect; they were reasonably priced and ran eight weeks. Doris decided to start taking some courses to improve herself and get a night out of the house.

There were all different classes such as oil painting, chair caning, sewing and cake decorating. She recruited some of her neighborhood girlfriends to join her. Out of necessity, they all chose beginner sewing to start. We got our picture in the local newspaper that year because Doris had made the most beautiful Easter suit for me. I was five years old and I remember it was a soft, baby pink wool. The jacket had a little Peter Pan collar, and the skirt was cut on the bias and to add fullness to already hide my chubby middle. I was so proud of my mother and how she could accomplish anything she put her mind too.

Sewing was probably the most successful course that Doris took. It allowed her to alter clothing that people gave us, and she was a genius at turning boy's coats into a girl's by reversing the buttonholes. She could take a good lining from a worn-out jacket and replace it into one that still had some life left in it. The courses that she took for pure pleasure are the ones that I remember most of all.

Oil Painting

Throughout my childhood, I felt that my mother and father were not very happy with their marriage. I once asked her if they had a happy marriage because if it was, I would hate to witness one that was on the rocks. Doris just laughed and said, "Sometimes you have to do what you have to do." She took courses so she could take out her frustration or escape to another world, even if it was only for a few hours out of a day.

This particular September, Doris took beginner oil painting. I remember laughing when she told us, because the only real piece of art we owned was a 16×20-inch ocean scene in oils that she had received as a wedding gift. The rest of the house was decorated in paint-by-number quality pictures and photos of real art. Also, I don't think she had really thought this one out, because oil paint and canvas were expensive, and our family really didn't have a lot of discretionary income. Doris' solution was to become a mural painter and use our tiny 6×6-foot bathroom as her canvas. The room had a white sink and toilet on the left and a white cast iron porcelain tub on the right. The walls and ceiling were bare except for a small medicine chest over the sink, and everything was already painted white. What more could she want?

Every Tuesday, Doris and two neighbors went to the Peabody High School for their class. Every Wednesday when she found a few spare hours, she would take her new paints and practice what she had learned the previous night. First, she started around the tub area with an ocean motif. Doris' waves were dark blue and black with white caps, and they swirled in every direction. It looked like a whirlpool just growing up from the tub. Then came a small wooden rowboat off the rocky shore, that in proportion to the water, made the waves look 20 feet high, and the little boat tossed around in the sea. None of this mattered: my mother was creating something unique, and it was making her happy.

The second week of the course brought farm life with corn silos and farm animals, all set in the fall foliage scenery of New England. I went to use the bathroom one afternoon and thought she was putting an authentic lighthouse on the Maine coast only to come back a few hours later to have an over scaled red barn with corn silo, grass and wheat fields falling off the rocky cliffs into the sea. At one point while I sat on the toilet staring at her creation and the crashing surf, I became seasick.

In the third week, she started painting flowers and a still life motif of a bowl of fruit. Doris had enough sense to know that a fruit bowl didn't belong in a mural of different landscape scenes, so she went for stand-alone flowers. Picture the wall behind the toilet with billowing wheat fields and twelve-inch sunflowers and tulips. They looked as though a few garden flowers had been exposed to radiation and mutated.

After a few days of admiring her work, Doris felt the sunflowers were a bit large in scale, so she decided all tulips would work better and she was much better at painting them. I was just starting to get used to the multi-colored tulips when I walked in and couldn't believe what she had done. Doris felt that she had done so well with her silo that she needed a windmill to match her tulips. The problem was that she didn't paint the familiar windmill from Holland. This was a Portuguese windmill. Instead of a pointed top it was dome-shaped like the Vatican. The body was painted white and the dome was bright red. The blades were like a checkerboard pattern with red along the top edges only. It was all very logical to Doris, and only Doris.

Last but not least came the week of the mountains and forests that we were so familiar with from camping for many years in Maine and New Hampshire. Unfortunately, her mountains were different. Try to picture Mt. Everest in the middle of some New England foothills. Doris lacked depth perception and the entire concept of scale when it came to tree sizes. The trees she created were not typical trees for such high elevations or mountaintops. The typical 300-foot redwood of California is not usually on top of a mountain. It was like placing ten-inch tapered candles on your average birthday cake: overkill. We are all still confused as to which forest has willow trees. We think that might have been in her consciousness due to the large willow tree on her campsite in Maine, so she threw one in for the hell of it. To Doris' stream of consciousness, it was a tree, wasn't it?

Her oil painting class was the longest 8 weeks the family had to endure. Unfortunately, the mural that Doris created had to stay even longer, at least two years. My mother was aware that it was offensive to the senses, but she just didn't have the money to cover it. The carpenters that came said the oil paints were all different thicknesses and would have to be sanded, primed and covered with two coats of paint. Doris' logic was if it was going to be so expensive to just repaint, why not save up and modernize with new fixtures and vanity? One thing that my mother could do was save money.

Two years after the mural began, it was covered in white ceramic bathroom tiles. They were arranged in a diamond pattern on the wall behind the new sink vanity and ceiling with an occasional yellow, pink, blue and green one put on for a bit of color.

The rest of the walls in the room were 4×4 inch white tiles in the traditional square pattern. Only the floor varied from this theme and was made up of tiny 2×2 inch tiles of white and very pale yellow. For those long two years that we waited for our bathroom makeover, Doris' mural was the talk of the neighborhood with weekly tours of the masterpiece that she had created. My only regret was that no one had the forethought to take some before-and-after pictures to have and possibly frame to show the world an original "Doris."

Ceramics

Doris learned her lesson with the oil painting class. The other ladies in the neighborhood were also not that artistic, so the next class had to be something easier, like ceramics. How hard can that be? You pick out a bowl, Christmas tree or water picture, then clean, paint and fire it and you have a masterpiece. That would have been the case if this class involved ready-formed greenware ceramics. Once again, my mother forgot to read the description of the class thoroughly; she saw the word ceramic and missed the sculpt-your-own-masterpiece-out-of-clay section. They were taking a sculpture class, not the ceramics that they had assumed it was.

The good part of this course is that there was no homework. Due to all the steps involved in taking a raw piece of clay to a finished product, there would only be two pieces for the course, which meant we had to wait in anticipation for four-weeks to see what Doris had created. I was a little nervous, and she wouldn't give any hints as to what she was working on.

Doris had completed her fourth week of class and assured us her creation would be coming home that night. She walked into the front hall around 9:15 P.M., but all she had was her purse.

Where was it? My mother opened her purse and brought out a piece of cloth that obviously had something wrapped in it. Finally the unveiling: there sat a three-dimensional figure of some sort, approximately eight inches tall, flesh colored at least at the top, and more browns at the lower half. What was it? Was it a human figure or perhaps some sort of small animal? The problem was that Doris herself wasn't sure what it was. We decided it was a piece of modern impressionism, "What you see is what it is."

For the second half of the class, Doris felt she would play it safe. The topic was an animal of your choosing. Doris decided a nice flat one-dimensional fish would be about her speed. Something told me from comments she made after her classes that her instructor was not impressed by her comic or artistic ability in his class, but he tolerated her presence. Since Doris was afraid of the ocean and never learned to swim, what fish could she possible choose? She had never gone to the aquarium in Boston to see all the colorful tropical varieties of fish. She only had the ones she consumed as a reference. I was not surprised that she chose to create a flat, grey flounder.

Doris kept working on her fish each week and at the last class could hardly wait to see it fired and completed. Suddenly the instructor entered the class and he appeared agitated and was heading straight toward my mother. Poor Doris, all she could think was her fish blew up in the kiln and ruined everyone else's projects. When he got to her workstation, he calmly looked her straight in the eyes and said, "Doris, this is very important. What color did you paint the fish?" She was taken aback and replied, "What?" Unfortunately, she had no clue what colors she had used. Doris was never one to follow instructions or recipes. She just mixed a little of this and a little of that.

Then out from the instructor's back came this fish. This time, it actually looked like a fish but that was not the problem. When people in the class saw it, there was a communal gasp. It was approximately ten-inches long and five-inches wide, but it was not grey or brown; the miracle was that it was bronzed. It looked as though it had been dipped in bronze like baby shoes or the statues in the town square. How did she do it?

Doris' poor teacher could see dollar signs and all that money going up in smoke. He begged her to please try to remember what colors she used and in which order. She didn't have the best memory, but she could see how desperate the teacher was. As she thought out loud, it was brown as the base coat and then copper, or was it gold, and I just kept adding colors, and I'm so sorry, but I don't know. The process that took ordinary ceramic paint and turned a piece of fired clay to bronze was lost forever.

Doris was not as upset as her instructor was. She was only glad that this time it looked like what she tried to make, a fish. The fact that it was bronze was just an added benefit. Unfortunately, on her return home that night, and haste to get through the front door, Mr. Fish came to an untimely end. He slipped out of her hand, hit the floor, and split in half. My brother Toney was happy and continued to play with the front half. The rest of the family was thrilled that we could identify what it was this time. One thing that you could count on when Doris took a class was that she came home in a good mood, and we were guaranteed a laugh out of her accomplishments.

Cake Decorating

The following year, Doris had learned her lesson and decided to stick with something she knew. She was good at cooking, so she chose cake decorating. I'm not sure where she got the idea since she did not excel in baking of any kind and definitely not pastry. Except for her world-renowned cream puffs, and cookies my mother really didn't bake anything. I think it had to do with presentation issues. Doris could cook multiple main dishes and they always tasted superb, but they were usually served from the pot they were created in, with no thought about presentation. Her reasoning was that she could create fun cakes for our birthdays for the cost of a cake mix and some confectionary sugar, so she was off. Doris had a plan.

Once again, she went to her first class where they gave out a list of necessary supplies and where to purchase them. The main item was the cake-decorating tool that resembled an oversized hypodermic syringe without the needle. There were specific tips that were used to create all the fancy designs and roses for the cakes. Doris had not taken into account the cost of these weekly items, such as shaped baking pans, and a metal pedestal holder to create her flowers on and it began to add up. It didn't matter to my mother; she focused on all the money she was going to save over the years on fancy birthday cakes, with the masterpieces that she would create herself.

On our refrigerator was the seven-week syllabus of which cake would be created each week and what had to be prepared at home and brought to class that night. Oh no, here we go again, homework. There were two simple frosting recipes: one was used to cover the cake in a base coat; the second type was the consistency needed to make roses, leaves, and all the spirals and swirls of the actual decorating component.

Week 2 was the patriotic Forth of July Stars and Stripes Forever cake, which was made as the basic 9×13 rectangle, baked in one of Doris lasagna pans, no cost there. There was a small cost for the two tips needed: one to create the actual stars and another for the fancy regulation stripes. Doris left with her rectangular cake all covered in the white base frosting, and we couldn't wait for the end results to come back. From what witnesses said, who had actually seen the cake when she left the school, it was perfect. At the end of our street, it went through a slight alteration when the driver had to stop abruptly to avoid another car. My mother ended up with the cake plastered to her chest. This was before seat belts were standard in cars and babies still traveled in car beds. Car travel was very dangerous back then, and it proved deadly for one poor cake.

We all ran to the door in time to witness Doris step out of the front seat and remove the cake from her bust line. Oh no, was it still edible? The cake was a little dented, but there were at least four stripes left intact. The stars had not been as fortunate and only the original 13 colonies had survived. I am here to tell you that it was still edible and delicious. All we could say was better luck next week.

Week four was a special cake for me: the doll cake. To create this cake, which was a woman in a ball gown, you baked the batter in a large round stainless steel bowl, and turned it over and the gown was complete. The woman was actually an inexpensive plastic Barbie look-alike without any clothing. Once the base coat was on the cake, Doris gently impaled her plastic doll into the center and it was ready to decorate at class.

Doris picked my favorite color, yellow, to decorate the cake. It was a relatively easy pattern made of little dabs of frosting using the star tip. She started at the base going around and around, and then frosted the doll body and the shoulders to create the top of the gown. I waited anxiously in the front window for my mother's return. To this day, we weren't sure if the problem had been the smooth texture of the doll or if Doris didn't make the frosting stiff enough. Whatever the reason was, by the time Doris walked up the front stairs of the house, she was carrying an X-rated doll cake. The frosting on the doll's body had slid down, landing like a shapeless lump around its waist leaving a very naked, anatomically correct female doll. Doris' partners in crime swore that her cake was one of the most beautiful cakes made that night. Once again, the cake was devoured after the doll was removed.

Week 8 finally arrived, and Doris made the most complicated cake to date, Big Bird from Sesame Street. This cake was going to be a yellow confectionary masterpiece. It was a simple concept, buy the special Big Bird pan, use the instructions for what colors and tips to use, and perfection. Unfortunately, in Doris' case, things didn't always go the way she planned, even when her intentions were honorable.

The secret of creating this popular children's character was to get the soft, light yellow color of the feathers and light blue for the eyes correct. The three balloons he was holding in his hand could be any primary color. Doris started to have problems from the start, her yellow was more a brownish yellow similar to Guldens spicy brown mustard. Her technique of making small uniform dabs of frosting was great at the head, but as she worked down the body, the dabs got larger as the bird got wider. Instead of the illusion of feathers, it looked more like bird droppings.

Doris' color choice for the eyes was a dark blue, almost black resembling Burmese sapphires, and they were hollow and lifeless. The eyes were larger than scale, and they encompassed the entire head, giving Big Bird a crazed appearance. The beak was made up of five large plops of frosting and resembled a bulbous nose rather than a sleek beak. The balloons were basic red, green and blue circles above his head because she forgot the line of white frosting for the strings that connected them to his hand. Yet they were probably the only things on the cake that were recognizable. The cake was brought home and hidden in my grandmother's refrigerator upstairs until the birthday party for Toney the next afternoon.

Finally, the party was in progress, and it was time for the unveiling of the cake and singing of Happy Birthday. I accompanied my mother upstairs to retrieve the cake, that I hadn't even seen yet. Doris pulled it off the shelf in the fridge and placed it on the kitchen table so that the candles could be appropriately placed. Apparently, my face told the whole story because Doris asked, "What do you think?" After some hesitation I said, "OH MY GOD MOM!" It looked like some diabolical prehistoric bird from hell; it was going to scar the children for life.

What to do now? Doris put on the appropriate number of candles and sent me downstairs to turn off the kitchen lights to set the mood. Down she came carrying this terrifying cake that was guaranteed to cause nightmares. It was a quick rendition of Happy Birthday, by subdued lighting and quick removal of the cake to the counter to start cutting, and covering the body parts with ice cream. Thankfully the children never really got a good look at the cake. Once they started to eat it, it was delicious, it just lacked artistic presentation.

The course ended and I don't recall Doris making anymore "special" cakes for us over the years. There was the year Toney wanted a green cake so she took a recipe for a red velvet cake and added green food coloring. The batter started emerald green and after baking, it was black. Thankfully six-year-olds go for taste, not looks. Only problem was that the green food color metamorphosed after being eaten. It transformed 12 children's bowel movements to emerald green for 48 hours. Once Doris called every child at the party's mother and explained the food-coloring incident, everything was well with the world.

There was only one other time that I can recall her trying her hand at creating another theme cake, and that was for a friend in 1971. One of our neighbors had 11 children, and her son was graduating from High School. He had been the co-captain of the winning football team and he was responsible for the end of the year party. They had no problem with the location since there yard was enormous and there were definitely enough tables and chairs, but cooking was not Mrs. Smith's forte. She elicited the help of the best cook that she knew: Doris.

Cooking to Doris was an act of love. She never refused anyone when they asked for help, and a woman who had 11 children needed all the help she could get. Anyone who could be pregnant 11 times, clean, do laundry and just remember all the children's names was an icon in Doris' mind.

The theme was all Royal Blue football paraphernalia and an outside garden buffet, not a cookout. Doris had gone over the menu with Mrs. Smith because the budget was a concern, as well as feeding 50 hungry, growing, teenage boys. Other parents on the team were also pitching in with paper products, drinks and desserts. Doris was only responsible for the main course and feeding approximately 75–100 people. This included the football team, parents, coaches and school faculty involved with the athletic program.

Doris should have kept to the main course, but somewhere along the way she felt a football shaped cake was appropriate to commemorate a winning season. She asked, "How hard could a little brown pigskin be to make, and decorate?" We all knew that it was harder than she thought.

The day arrived, and the weather was perfect, sunny and warm. The yard was decorated, food had been cooked and delivered, and Doris went home to finish up her surprise! The yellow cake was baked and turned out of the 9×16 pan without any mishaps, but then came the frosting. Right away the brown color was wrong; it was milk chocolate instead of the dark rich brown of an espresso. With a football on the counter next to her for inspiration, she cut out the shape that would be the cake. All she had to do was cut out an oval, but instead it was more tube-like and resembled a sub or grinder roll. My brother and I begged her to abandon the surprise and not embarrass herself with this thing that she called her pigskin, but our pleas went unheeded.

Doris completed her decorating and received a call to let her know that the meal was completed and the desserts were being served. She picked up the cake and drove the two streets back to the party. I accompanied her because I knew there was cleanup involved, and I had to see the expression on these teenage boy's faces when she presented her masterpiece to them. All smiles, Doris walked into the back yard and everyone came over to compliment her on the meal she had created. Then they saw it.

What was it suppose to be? It was a 13-in long, milk chocolate brown, hoagie roll with white stripes. Her attempt at making the white laces left these white stripes across the entire cake instead of just at the top. There was the monogram of SJP in a dark navy blue on either side of the stripes, a last-minute impulse. I think that is when the shock of this thing, sitting in the center of these beautiful desserts hit everyone. Suddenly there was a roar of laughter and one brave football player yelled, "It's a football."

Thank God everyone had just sampled Doris' ability to cook so Dan decided that since he was the host, he would be the guinea pig. He cut the cake and tasted the first piece. If you didn't look at it while you were eating, it was actually light and fluffy, and the frosting was buttery and delicious. Once again, my mother's heart was in the right place, all that she lacked was visual presentation.

Doris the Builder

I learned at a very young age that you never tell Doris she can't do something or dare her because sometimes the results could be dangerous. Every year or two with the tax return money, Doris would plan a remodeling project in our little four-room apartment. Usually, my father would hire some hacker who did remodeling on the side, and worked cheap. Doris would always end up hiring a real tradesman later to fix the mistakes of my father's friends. After two fiascos, one involving the wainscoting in the living room, and built-in bookshelves in the kid's bedroom, she had learned her lesson. Doris would take on the kitchen herself.

Dream Kitchen

My grandparents purchased the two-story house we lived in, in 1924 for $1,100. It was considered a two family with three rooms in each unit, but it lacked indoor plumbing. A bathroom was added at the top of the second floor stairs around 1933 and was shared by both families. In 1948, when Doris announced she was getting married, my grandfather decided his only daughter would live on the first floor. She would need a new master bedroom, private bath and designer kitchen.

A builder was hired and plans developed to add on a two-story addition. There would be two new bedrooms, one for Doris on the first floor, and directly above it in my grandparents apartment on the second floor. A small bath was placed under the new back staircase, and a new kitchen with custom cabinets and new appliances was designed and built.

Doris was already in love with anything made of wood. The cabinets were to be made of knotty pine in a plain flat-front door style, with black wrought iron, H&L hinges to add a rustic charm. More pine was added three quarters of the way up the walls for a custom vertical wainscoting. Everything was stained in a deep red cherry finish, since in the 1940s the dark woods, cherry, walnut and mahogany, were the rage.

My grandfather was a practical man, so the size of the bedroom was modest. It had two windows on opposing walls for proper cross ventilation. Doris asked her father to have the cabinetmaker build closets and cabinets all along the bed wall and have the bed fit into the center. Daddy's girl convinced him of the practicality of it, and she designed two five foot tall, his and hers closets on either side of the bed. She added five large built-in cabinets across the ceiling and over the bed to capitalize on the limited space. Doris was ahead of her time on organization.

Approximately 20 years later, Doris decided to redo her kitchen. The lighter woods like maple and oak were popular, and the woodwork had really darkened over the years. Doris decided to let my father in on her plan and his reaction was, "You can't possibly do that yourself. When are you going to find the time?

You're crazy." Big mistake on his part, because even I knew to never dare Doris that she can't do something. She was the most stubborn, self-motivated and organized person I knew and know to this day.

Doris went into action. She was wise enough to know that she would have to hire a carpenter for the new counters and a plumber for the new sink and dishwasher, but the rest she was convinced that she could handle. What did her part of the remodel project include? Removing 16 cabinet doors from the frames and carrying them, with six drawers, to the basement. There were the cabinet frames and over 250 square feet of wainscoting on the walls that had to be stripped and refinished in place. Once all this wood was stripped, it had to be sanded, and four coats of satin polyurethane applied. There was hand sanding between each coat to achieve the look and appearance of fine furniture. Doris never did anything "half assed."

First, she had to have a plan. Since my mother had never refinished anything in her life, she needed to speak to the experts, so off she went to the local hardware store. In the 60s and 70s there were no super stores like Home Depot or Lowes, so you had to depend on the independently owned neighborhood hardware store for supplies and instructions. Conveniently, there was a store two blocks away, actually within walking distance. She explained her plan and was loaded up with one electric sander, boxes of sand paper in multiple grits, paint brushes, and gallons and gallons of Stripese (varnish remover).

Phase One was to remove any door or piece of wood that could be brought to the basement and refinish it there. Doris decided to start with these pieces first and set up an assembly line to strip, sand and refinish. Once Phase One was completed, she would move upstairs to the actual kitchen. At this time, we were spending a lot of our summers in Maine, so her project time was limited to a few hours here and there. Thus began the two-year-plus kitchen remodel project. We lived without cabinet doors and the contents of our kitchen exposed for the entire world to see for what seemed like forever.

Finally, Doris entered Phase Two: the wooden wainscoting on the walls in the actual kitchen. There was a light at the end of the tunnel. I can assure you from living with my mother for over 25 years, I don't think that Doris ever read the instructions, on any product thoroughly, before using it. I wondered if all the Stripese fumes in the basement had caused some minor brain damage and this was responsible for her behavior. When she started with the kitchen, she went after the largest wall, approximately eight feet wide and five feet tall, and was located behind our table and five chairs. In this four-room apartment, we didn't have a formal dining room. We ate all our meals in the kitchen, so the set was moved to the small living room, which served double duty as TV/dining room for months.

Doris had a plan; open all windows wide for proper ventilation, children all out for the day at neighbor's homes, and she was ready to begin. She began the grueling task of applying a thick coating of the chemical stripper, waiting the 20 minutes for it to work and then carefully scraping off the finish, and repeat. Since the wood paneling was tongue and groove, the pieces were all different widths and Doris chose a two inch metal scrapper to fit the narrower piece so she would avoid gouging the wood.

Doris thought she had covered all the potential problems, but she forgot one very important thing: Stripese is highly FLAMMABLE. It just so happened that the only light switch in the entire kitchen, to the one overhead light fixture, was located on her test wall. Doris didn't want to take a chance of ruining her new brass switch plate so she had removed it for safe keeping, and that left the metal switch box exposed.

The overhead light was on so she could see what she was doing and Doris had already applied the first coat of remover.

Now it was time to scrape it off. Doris went up the wall with her metal putty scrapper, caught the edge of the metal electrical box and KABOOM. A tiny spark from the metal hitting metal had ignited the entire wall into blue flames. Doris was in a state of shock for a second, but thank God, instinct took over.

The only phone in the entire house was located on the opposite wall next to the sink. Doris was able to call the fire department, dial the seven-digit number and calmly give her address, since it was well before the automated 911 systems. The reason for her call was that her kitchen was on fire. While on the phone she was able to multi-task and kept refilling the dishpan in the sink and throwing water at the wall engulfed in flames.

The closest firehouse was only 300 yards away, and the fire engine was at the front door within minutes, with lights flashing and sirens blasting. Teodolinda, her mother got the surprise of her life when she came downstairs to see what all the commotion was and ran into two firefighters coming through the front door carrying very large axes. The adrenaline was definitely pumping through Doris' veins because when she saw the axes and the looks of "Let me at it" on the faces of firefighters, she stared to yell, "STOP, STOP." Covered in soot and smoke swirling around the room, she yelled again, "Don't you dare touch my kitchen. The fire is out."

Doris had single handedly started and put out a fire in 5 minutes, but she was still left with a big mess. The fire had been superficial; the chemical was actually what was burning, but it did manage to do damage to her beautiful wood paneling. Also, even though Doris knew two of the firemen from high school, she had to let them take down the wall to make sure there was no fire trapped inside. They were as careful as possible because they didn't want to have to endure, the wrath of Doris.

The aftermath left Doris with a dilemma: how would she ever be able to match the wood paneling to the rest of the kitchen? It was only one wall so maybe brick would work. We didn't have a fireplace in the house, and brick would make the room cozy. My mother wasn't crazy enough to try and have a mason start a new wall. No, she was thinking of artificial brick. Doris had been out selling raffle tickets for the bizarre when she stopped at Mrs. Wilson's house, in the Gardner Park section of town. She saw a beautiful, white brick wall in Mrs. Wilson's new kitchen. Doris picked up the phone and called her and asked about the wall. She assured her it was very reasonably priced. Doris removed all the remaining wood from the wall and decided fake brick was the way to go.

Doris was once again a little premature in her actions. She had not taken into consideration that reasonably priced to someone in a four room apartment might not mean the same thing to a woman in a 12-room, center-entry colonial with attached two car garage. My mother called the contractor and received the bad news. The so-called reasonably priced brick was $200 a sheet, and she needed two sheets plus installation for the grand total of $600. The good news was that the insurance money would cover most of it and the savings on the Stripese alone, for that wall would make up the difference.

Approximately six months later, the entire kitchen was completed. The cabinets and wooden wainscoting were all a natural golden color and all the distress of the years just added to their charm. We had a beautiful single bowl, white porcelain sink and an actual garbage disposal. The new counter was a white-on-white leaf pattern Formica and was perfect. The floor was a new linoleum product called Congolium, and my mother and I chose a federal blue with a silvery white geometric pattern. It was so hip. The three-foot walls above the wood paneling had always been painted, but with the light color of the cabinets, white brick wall, Doris felt wallpaper was in order. We went to the wallpaper store and I gave my input. We chose an octagonal-shaped design in yellow, pale blue, white and a hint of red on a background of federal blue. Finally, the new appliances were added, including our first Kitchen Aid dishwasher and side-by-side refrigerator freezer, all in the fashionable Harvest gold. We were all so proud of Doris and the job she had done. Even my father had to eat crow.

Doris' kitchen was all finished, but there was still one thing missing on the white brick wall. My mother was never one to copy something someone else had done or try and keep up with the Jones, because she knew we couldn't, yet she had loved the way Mrs. Wilson had decorated her wall. There were five copper pots and pans hung from black wrought iron hooks, and they completed the look.

Months went by and Doris was constantly searching for the perfect items to hang on her brick wall. By this time, we didn't camp in Maine anymore because the trailer had been sold for money to start my brother in private high school. Doris was now working full time as a bookkeeper with her major goal to provide her children with the best education she could afford. One Saturday morning my mother and I decided to drive to Maine for the day, along old Route One and shop. We had no particular items in mind, but there was the old Trading Post and a lot of craft and furniture stores, and we thought it would be fun.

Things had changed dramatically in the two years that we no longer made the weekly journey to Maine. The Maine turnpike was completed and getting to our old campground took less time. Doris was never one to drive on the highways; she always preferred the slower scenic routes and Route One had so many retail stores. We saw this sign for a woodworking store up ahead, so I pulled in.

Doris was in heaven; everything was made of wood. There were solid wooden salad bowl sets, stained in rich browns and gold tones that brought out their grains. She spotted a large fork and spoon set, approximately 18 inches long, hung on the wall. She thought of her "brick wall," but the price was $25, too expensive. I felt badly for my mother. I could tell how excited she was when she saw them, but her children came first, so they were left in the store.

We had gotten into the car to leave, and the parking lot was overflowing with cars. I couldn't back out onto a major road, so I decided to turn around at the back of the store. It was like a dream come true: this mound of wooden unstained bowls, and wooden spatulas that would be turned into the forks and spoons. Why were they outside? I could see Doris' mind start clicking, and she got out of the car and began picking through the pile. We went back into the store carrying the wooden pieces. The salesman came up to her and asked, "Where did you get the reject forms from?" Doris answered, "From the pile in the back yard. Are they for sale?"

The man had a confused look on his face. He explained that they were the seconds, bowls with hairline cracks so they couldn't be used for salad bowls, and the spatulas had knots, which made turning them into forks impossible, so they were scraped. Doris didn't want to eat out of them, she wanted to hang them on her wall. Once again she asked, "Can I buy them? I want you to stain them, put handles on the bowls with a hole drilled through the end, so that I can hang them on my brick wall." It took the salesman a few minutes to grasp what Doris was proposing and then he understood. Since the scraps were sold for firewood, he charged her $3 for each bowl and $2 for the pair of spatulas. She also located a peppershaker on a long handle that had a crack, and he threw it in for the grand total of $10.

Doris had gone back out after he agreed to her proposition to go through the pile and get the best of the seconds. She knew her woods, and she looked for ones with unusual grain patterns that the stain would highlight. The following week, we arrived to pick up our treasures. The salesman was amazed at how beautiful they had come out. Now that they had a handle and a place for the rawhide to go through, he could understand her plan.

When we got home that day, Doris was so happy. Why hadn't she thought of it before this? It had taken seeing that pile of wooden bowls to trigger her idea and a $25 price tag on the fork and spoon. Doris had purchased the same black wrought iron hooks that Mrs. Wilson had used, for the two bigger bowls. Smaller brass hooks to match her brass switch plate, were hung for the lightweight items.

Years later, when shopping malls and outlet stores began to spring up in York, Maine, we once again went up Route One for a shopping spree. We revisited our favorite wood shop, and to our surprise, there were Doris' bowls with handles all over the walls. They weren't selling for $3 each. They had taken Doris' idea and turned their seconds into a number one moneymaker. I was upset to think she came up with the idea and didn't get anything for it. Then I was reminded that she got an entire brick wall decorated for the bargain price of $10. Doris was happy.

Wooden Ceilings

In the early 1970s, our city built an ice skating rink on the property adjacent to the new Peabody High School. My brothers had always loved skating and playing ice hockey and this was a dream come true. The only rinks that were available prior to this were quite a distance away and playing time was usually in the wee hours of the night. It was around this time that my younger brother joined a city team, and Doris' life would never be the same.

Doris found herself sitting in the beautiful A-framed facility day in and day out. She wore her black, fur-lined boots and winter ski parka due to the frigid temperatures inside the rink. On one occasion during a very early morning practice, she found herself getting a little bored. My mother didn't have any hobbies such as reading or knitting that she could do while she waited, so she usually just watched the kids skate. This particular day she found herself staring up at the beautiful, tongue and groove, wide plank pine ceiling with the polyurethane finish. It was love at first sight. It must have been around tax return time, because that year's project was going to be low key: sand and paint the ceilings of our apartment, all four of them. Now her mind was racing, why just paint when you could cover over all of them with this beautiful natural wood?

There were limitations to her carpentry ability, and she knew she would need to hire someone to actually hang the wooden planks, but we all knew she was an expert on finishing them. Good old Dad worked with a guy who was willing to nail it up, only he had no way to get the lumber to the house or the time to polyurethane it. He suggested a lumberyard that had good quality product, and to sand and finish all the boards prior to his installation.

Doris called the lumberyard that was recommended to see about cost and if they had free delivery. Apparently, there was a minimum purchase amount before delivery was free, otherwise it was based on miles traveled. Unfortunately, when the price of the job was computed, there would be a cost of $100 to deliver the lumber to our home in Peabody. "Forget it" she said. That $100 delivery fee was money that could be used to pay the carpenter to hang it. We owned a maroon Ford station wagon at that time, and the backseat folded down. "So why can't we get the wood ourselves?" she asked. So we did.

I stopped counting the number of trips back and forth to the lumberyard before we actually had all the lumber stacked in the side of our driveway. The planks were tongue and groove and could be used on either side, wide or graduated widths, and all were 10 feet long. Doris had her heart set on the wide plank look, and the next day we started at first light with "The Doris Brown Wood Refinishing Assembly Line" set up in the driveway and garage. Thank God all that the wood required was a gentle hand sanding to get any rough spots off, tack off with turpentine and one or two coats of satin polyurethane.

My mother had borrowed every sawhorse, folding table and chair, and anything that anyone in the neighborhood owned that a 10-foot plank could dry on. Every piece went through the first station; it was a long table where the plank was sanded and wiped clean and then carried by two volunteers to a drying station. There the polyurethane was applied in place. Doris didn't want them touched once the finish was on, risking a chance of smudges. God was with her those four days because the weather was in the low 70s, dry and no wind. It was perfect weather conditions for outdoor painting. Also, we just roped off the end of the driveway and left everything there to dry overnight.

Doris would decide after the first coat had dried for 24 hours, if we needed to do it all over again. Unfortunately, the quick one-hour drying polyurethanes didn't exist yet. It would have made our lives so much easier if they had. One thing that she did do that night was read all the labels on the cans of chemicals that we would use. Doris wasn't taking any chances of history repeating itself in the garage, especially since it was attached to the house.

It took four days to complete the project since Doris did require the second coat of polyurethane because once the boards were on the ceiling, it would be so much more difficult for "US" to put on another coat. I thank her today because I would have been the "US" bent over backward on a ladder doing the second coat. My mother actually lucked out with my father's choice of carpenter. He was able to hang all four room ceilings and one 4×4 hallway over the next three weekends. The only glitch he ran into was trying to hang the six-inch-wide outdoor cove molding that Doris had chosen for the living room. The bay window was rounded at the corners, as well as out of square. The house was only 80 plus years old. It took the 70-year-old, retired, Italian carpenter from next door, Mario, to get it to fit using years of experience and talent. All the ceilings are still there today; after 40 years, no warping or loose boards, and the finish has never had to be redone.

Doris doesn't take on the big physical remodeling jobs anymore. Now she's interested in interior decorating. She recently stenciled around her bedroom ceiling, doing a little every other day until she was finished. She doesn't file income taxes any longer. I think she misses the tax return money, and all the plans that she would make on how she would spend it. Today Doris says, "I finally have the house just the way I want it, so why mess with perfection?"

Bunny Hutch

My brothers and I had always wanted a pet, only to be told that my older brother had a bird when he was little, but he was allergic to feathers and the bird was given away. Part of it could have been my father's hatred of all animals. He would always say, "You People, get a pet, dog, cat, doesn't matter, I'm out of here." Unfortunately, in 1970 we called his bluff and bought a pure white, pink-eyed, albino bunny for Easter, and he didn't leave.

We quickly named this one-pound ball of fur, Fluffy. It wasn't very original, but it made my baby brother Toney happy. She answered to the name immediately. Fluffy was kept in a tall cardboard box in the corner of the kitchen until she began to grow and could jump out. We treated her like one of the family lying in bed with us and on the couch watching television. In nice weather, we had a collar and leash and we took her for walks around the neighborhood.

The problem with Fluffy was that she was supposed to be a dwarf rabbit, no larger than three pounds when she reached maturity. Fluffy was approaching five months old, and she kept getting bigger and bigger, eating pellets, carrots and her favorite, chocolate-covered ice creams bars. Her final weight was 11 pounds, and she resembled a large house cat. Doris knew it was time to put our baby outside to live while it was still summer and she could build up a thick coat of fur to survive the winter.

That was a great concept, but where was she going to stay and in what? Our backyard was approximately 50×50 feet, and it already had a 6×8 foot tool shed in the far corner. A friend had given us a 2×3 foot bottomless wire cage that we would put over her in the yard so she was able to frolic in the lawn and not run away. One morning out of the blue, Doris made a statement, "We need a bunny hutch."

The dilemma was where does one buy a bunny house? The only time we went to the pet store was to buy her the 50-pound bag of rabbit pellets and wood shavings for the bottom of the box. We had never seen anything that looked like a house for a rabbit. Money was tight, and we needed a frugal solution to this problem. Doris was aware of an unfinished furniture store that boasted, if it could be made out of wood, they carried it.

The furniture store was enormous and two stories high. When we entered through the front door an old metal bell quivered announcing our arrival. A 60-year-plus balding salesman was at our side in an instant, and he asked, "How may I help you today?" Doris just said, "Bunny Hutch, please. Do you have them?"

They had a variety of animal houses. Dog houses in three styles; simple single-story cape; the usual A-frame; and the

Cadillac, a two story mansion with actual pillars flanking each side of the opening. Doris flashed me a smirk. I had this strange sensation after seeing what the doghouses looked like, what would a rabbit house cost?

There it was, the most beautiful house any rabbit would ever want. It was two stories high with an unpainted pine structure on the second level that had a flip-up roof on brass hinges for easy access and cleaning. The front had a small arch opening that led to a galvanized chicken wire front yard with a wooden ramp going down to the lower level. If it was placed on the lawn, the lower level resembled a Florida room. Fluffy could enjoy the nice weather without fear of any neighborhood predators.

Then Doris asked the dreaded question, "How much?" I said a quick prayer, "Please God, let it be cheap." The salesman fumbled for the paper price tag that hung from the side, there in black marker was $45. That was that. I knew that Fluffy was never going to enjoy these luxury accommodations at that price. At the time, $45 was two weeks groceries for the entire family.

Doris thanked the man for his time and said, "We have to think about it, and we'll get back to you." By the time we got to the red station wagon, my brother Toney was in tears. He was crying and asked, "Mommy, why can't we get the house for Fluffy? It was so pretty. I know she would love it." We all knew that the hutch was perfect; it was the cost that was the problem. Toney was still young enough not to understand the family's finances, and we didn't have the $45 to spend.

We were driving the 10 minutes to get home and there was dead silence in the car. It was though someone had died and we were in mourning, mourning the death of the hutch that could have been. Then Doris broke the silence, "How hard can it be to build a rabbit house? Some wood, nails, chicken wire and elbow grease, and you get a house." Oh no, she wasn't going to try and build it herself? I had witnessed my mother do a lot of things over the years, but build something out of wood? Doris knew how to sand and refinish wood, but nail pieces together and build something from scratch scared me.

We walked into our kitchen, and Doris immediately went to get paper and pencil to draw a sketch of the new Bunny Hutch before she forgot any of the details. She was able to draw something that did look right, but she had no measurements to know how big things were supposed to be. Doris' analogy was that she had altered many paper patterns to make clothing out of fabric. This was the same concept, only made with wood, metal and nails.

In the 70s, we had to rely on the neighborhood lumber/hardware store for guidance. There was no How to Classes on weekends to teach Doris how to build the Bunny Hutch. Over the years Doris had developed a relationship with the local hardware store. The owner once said, "The money I made on Doris' purchases of Stripese and sandpaper alone, sent my two children to college." When he saw Doris come through the door, paper in hand, he wondered what she had gotten herself into this time.

Doris was always trying to make the dollar stretch, so she had gone through the basement, garage and shed to locate anything we already had that could be used for the project and save money. We had pine framing lumber and a set of brass hinges for the roof. In her father's old workroom were jars of nails in all sizes and shapes. There were my grandfather's old hand tools; a hammer with its well-worn wooden handle, various saws to cut wood and metal, but no staple gun for the chicken wire. The only thing she needed was the plywood for the house, roofing shingles and the correct size chicken wire for Fluffy's little feet.

George at the hardware store was Doris' savior. He was able to take her sketch and give her dimensions that would do the entire house out of one 4×8 foot sheet of exterior plywood. Miraculously a cord of roofing shingles had broken apart in the store and he gave my mother a deal on the 14 shingles needed for the little roof. Aware of the square footage a roll of chicken wire could cover, he once again made the size of the front yard and lower level able to be completed by two rolls without any waste. Since my father was not handy around the house in any fashion, we owned no power tools. All the wood was going to be manually sawed, so Doris splurged on a hand-held staple gun to fasten all the chicken wire to the frame. With everything she needed in the car and a few instructions from George, we were on our way home to start.

George had given Doris a quick hand-written set of instructions: start with the bottom frame; build the house separately, then nail it to the frame; attach the ramp to the base of the house; finally add chicken wire to the entire structure; and paint. The house was approximately 2 feet wide, 3 feet long and 18 inches tall. Since Doris used a wooden yardstick for all her measurements, I say approximately. She had not been able to locate a carpenter's rule in the house and it was an unnecessary expense to buy one. She had a ruler and an inch was still an inch.

I was so proud of my mother when the Bunny Hutch was completed. It really looked like the one in the store except for a few changes. The original opening from the house to front yard had been an arch. Doris had to use a narrow hacksaw to make the cut and was better at sawing right angles, so the opening on her house was square. All the edges were sanded smooth so Fluffy was never in any danger of injury. Also, the hinges for the pop-up roof had been hidden inside the original house, but for some reason Doris' were on the outside. It was quickly resolved and hidden by the roofing shingles so no one even knew. We were just amazed that the roof actually opened and closed.

The final product was painted blue, which was my baby brother's choice, and Doris gave the boys the task of painting it. Fluffy was moved into her new accommodations in June. She really seemed to enjoy the house with its clean wood chips and access to the grass from her first floor patio. It was set up in the far corner of the yard next to the tool shed. Occasionally as a treat, she was still brought into the house to cuddle on the couch and watch T.V. She would still be taken for a walk on her leash, weather permitting. Due to her increasing size, she was put on a diet and the chocolate-covered ice creams had to be eliminated for lower calorie carrots.

Fluffy lived happily in her house that Doris had made for seven years. One day in February, my older brother went out to clean her house and feed her and found a frozen, bunny icicle. He came running into the house to tell our mother. How was Doris going to tell Toney and I that our baby was dead?

Later that afternoon, we were all in the kitchen and Doris was writing out the weekly grocery list. Toney came over and wrote carrots on the bottom of the paper and said, "Don't forget them, Mom. Fluffy needs her treats." She just walked over, and in Doris style, took the pencil and crossed out the word carrot from the list. There was a second of silence when we just looked at her, and then she said, "Poor Fluffy is gone." I asked, "Mom, define gone. Ran away? No, No, she isn't dead, is she?" Doris just shook her head in the affirmative and we all started to cry. There was a lot of hugging and crying until we finally went to her house to see our baby and say goodbye.

Later that week we learned that a total of four pets died within a seven day period. My cousin's Irish setter, the two cats up the hill and our Fluffy. All we could think was that there must have been some type of animal virus, because these animals were all healthy and didn't leave their houses or yards.

The weeks went on and Easter was fast approaching. We had all talked about the possibility of buying a new bunny and agreed there was no way to replace Fluffy. Where could we find a rabbit that liked to lie on the couch and watch T.V., never soiled in the house or bit anyone? Not to mention eating chocolate-covered ice cream bars while I held her like a baby in my arms.

We learned that one of the neighbors up the hill was getting the traditional white bunny for Easter, so we decided to give them the house. Doris had done such a quality job of building the bunny hutch that it was still in perfect condition. We all agreed it could maybe use a fresh coat of paint, but we would let the new owners do it. They might not like blue.

Doris The
Professional Volunteer

My memories of growing up with Doris were that she was always there. She was at the breakfast table and she tucked us into bed at night. Coming home in the afternoon, she would be at the house cooking dinner or getting ready to take us somewhere, Girl Scouts, Boy Scouts or some athletic practice. Doris was the poster child of the stay-at-home mom. I think if you asked my mother what she did for a living, she would say she was a bookkeeper. Ask her what she was, and she would say a mother.

Doris was very involved with every aspect of her children's lives. The private catholic schools we attended and going to college was her number one priority. Her father had always said, "Give your children an education and they can support themselves. Leave them money and someone can swindle them; then they have nothing." This was from a man who never learned to read or write. My grandfather encouraged my mother to go to a business school after high school so she would have a profession.

Doris didn't go back to the work force full time until my older brother started high school. She worked as a bookkeeper in a leather factory and also baked and sold 40 loaves of Portuguese sweet bread to her customers every weekend. Up until then, she was at every school function and was the first one to raise her hand whenever a volunteer was needed. Anything that she could do to help someone else, she did. Sometimes I think she felt she had to make up for our family's lack of money. Doris didn't have cash, but no one could stop her from donating her time and talents.

Over the years, Doris volunteered: being an assistant Girl Scout leader; acting as a Boy Scout merit badge counselor; cooking a special meal every month for the sisters of my grammar school; organizing school fundraisers; working the snack bar at my high school bingo night; and chaperoning multiple school field trips over the years. Doris had a belief that there were no bad children in the world, just bad parents. Her philosophy was that if you made the decision to give birth or adopt a child, they better be the center of your world. People should be willing to sacrifice material things to be with their kids. It's as simple as that.

Merit Badge Counselor

My older brother was part of the Boy Scout Troop at St. Thomas School for many years. They had two young leaders who were enthusiastic and wanted to see all the boys succeed and ultimately become Eagle Scouts. Jim was a 24-year-old married high school teacher who had a long family history of being involved in Boy Scouts. Ed was a 21-year-old single leader, and the two had been best friends since they had met in Boy Scouts.

Come Tuesday afternoon, you would find them all in the gymnasium of St. Thomas School for their weekly meeting. At its height of popularity, the troop had approximately 30 scouts. They organized field trips, hikes, community projects and camping trips. The goal was to meet the many requirements and move up the ladder from Tenderfoot to the top rank of Eagle Scout. At the time, there were over 100 merit badges to choose from. The leaders were very good, but they needed the help of some of the mothers and fathers to be in charge of certifying scouts for certain badges. Everyone had some hobby or profession that could qualify him or her as a merit badge counselor. Since my father's talents, golfing and bowling, weren't on the list, Doris volunteered her time as Junior's parent.

The scouts brought home a flyer that listed the 100 plus titles with some of the requirements of what had to be done. Being a professional organization, there were forms to fill out and sign. By signing the form, you took an oath that the boy had completed all the requirements according to the strict Boy Scout of America Standards. This was kind of scary to Doris because she really wasn't a regimented, follow-a-schedule type of person. In the C column of possible badges, just between coin collecting and cotton farming, was Cooking.

Doris called Jim to let him know that she might be interested in the cooking badge. He was thrilled because everyone knew the talents Mrs. Brown possessed in that particular area. Our parish was unique. It began over the line in Danvers to the west through Peabody, and the east side of the church was actually in Salem. It was important that the locations chosen be convenient for the boys to walk to or ride their bicycles. Since most of the boys lived within a mile or two of the school, Doris was hired, no references or background check required, and would start immediately.

Jim was so thrilled because cooking was a popular badge and relatively easy for a boy of any age to complete. Word spread that Brown's mother was doing cooking, and the calls started to flood in to set up appointments. Doris was given the brochure that had all the steps that had to be followed and completed. In the mail arrived the official paperwork that had to be filled in by her, signed and mailed back to the Boy Scout Counsel for approval.

There was only one glitch. Doris had once again failed to read all the fine print. All cooking had to be done outdoors, in a fire pit. Only government-issued mess kits and tin cans were allowed as the cooking implements. My mother didn't panic. Doris was the Queen of building the tee-pee-style fire. Also, we owned the vacant lot behind our house so there wouldn't be any damage to our beautiful backyard. Luckily, it was prior to the town regulations banning outdoor fires, so she was good to go.

Saturday arrived, and Doris had her first two victims. Tom was 12 and Mike 15, and they were going to be Doris' test case. My mother, still fearful of fire, had cleared a large area of any dry grass and brush. Doris had the green garden hose already pulled to the site, on, and primed. "Be prepared for anything." Wasn't that the Boy Scout motto?

The rules were as follows:

- Dig an open fire pit, 2 feet in diameter and 18 inches deep.
- Start fire using rock and flint. All fire wood had to be gathered by the scout.
- Use the government issued mess kit and tin cans only for cooking. The exception being a grate that was allowed over the pit. (This had been supplied to Doris by the troop)
- Prepare, cook and serve in a clean manner a meal for four people.
- This meal should be nutritious and include the four basic food groups, at a reasonable cost.
- Extinguish all fire and clean up the site and return it to its original state.

Doris did have a few problems sticking with the letter of the law. Since we had no wooded areas to allow the scout to go gather his firewood, Doris felt as long as the scout carried his own wood from the pile next to the shed, it was legitimate. On our first outing, the wood was a little damp and a wooden match had to be used to ignite the fire, but all evidence was burned. From that day on, Doris kept the wood covered and dry. There was never a problem with the four test tasters because my younger brother and I were always willing and available. I loved to eat and still do.

I was amazed that first day at what Mike had planned. The first course was baked tomato and cheese on a white bread crouton. The main course was a bone-in pork chop, topped with a pineapple slice and prune center. Dessert was a banana baked in its skin using a cleaned-out tin can. Meeting the four basic food groups, Mike had included a grain in the slice of white bread crouton. Protein was the thinly sliced pork chop, and slice of orange American cheese. The vegetable was the tomato that was part of the appetizer. I wasn't sure if it was actually supposed to have been considered a fruit. Finally, was the fruit group that had three selections: pineapple slice, prune and banana.

Troupe 94 scouts were always prepared and took this badge very seriously. The biggest problem that Doris ever encountered was to sit back and just observe. My mother was a hands-on person and it was almost impossible at times for her not to help chop, stir or serve. Also, the Boy Scout manual never said how to rate the meal after it was prepared. Doris felt if they completed the six steps, the food was edible and we were still alive the next day, they passed. She never had a failure.

At some point in their Boy Scout career, a boy would have to get by Doris on their quest for the Holy Grail, Eagle Scout. My older brother had just become a Life Scout when everything changed. A new pastor was assigned to St. Thomas Parish and he was on a dictator trip. Once he had reviewed the church finances, he stopped all the mother's and father's club activities and confiscated the bankbooks. What put Doris over the edge was when he wanted to start charging rent for the after-school groups to use the hall.

Needless to say, this was the beginning of the downfall of our church. The Boy and Girl Scout troops disbanded and the children joined other groups nearer to their homes. The Father alienated the young people of the parish, and that is when my brother and I started skipping Sunday mass. It wasn't much longer before the school was in financial ruin and had to close its doors.

During this era, the priests in the archdiocese of Boston belonged to an exclusive good old boys' club. All the letter writing from the parishioners to the archbishop fell upon deaf ears. Doris had a saying that she told us: "Priests are just men who wear dresses." We were taught to respect all clergy, only there was a hidden message from my mother, and she would say, "If any person, priest, police officer, or teacher ever makes you feel uncomfortable, go with your instincts and come right home and tell me." I always knew that she would believe me because Doris had built in radar, when it came to child predators.

Unfortunately, in the Boston archdiocese pedophile scandal of the early 2000s, St. Thomas Parish did not come out untouched. A priest that was there in the late 60s was accused of molesting one of the boys who happened to be in the troupe. The priest died before formal charges could be brought against him. When my mother learned about this on the news, she cried. Doris had never liked this particular priest and would tell my brother to come home right after boy scouts and not hang around in the school yard if Father was around.

In a round about way, the priests assigned to St Thomas over the years to help and guide us were ultimately the ones who destroyed it. In 2005, St. Thomas was on the list of churches to be closed and sold to gain money to pay off the massive priest pedophile settlement. It makes me sad every time I get to the top of my mother's street and face off with the front door of the church. As a teenager, I always had this thought about what it would feel like to keep driving up the stairs and through the front door. Being a chicken, I never came close to doing it. This church had been such an integral part of my life. Now it is only a sad reminder of both fun and sad times.

High School Cooking Teacher

From the day we were all born, Doris would keep telling us the most important thing is to get a good education and go to college. Choose a profession or trade that will give you a good living and something you love to do. In my case, she would throw in the need for a woman to have a profession that allows her to be financially independent. A woman never needs a man to be complete. Getting married and having a man in your life should always be a choice, not a necessity. I think part of it came from the fact that she was trapped in her marriage until we were old enough and she could return to work and support us on her own. Doris had always been a strong single mother in raising her children, but it became official on paper with the divorce from my father in 1975.

In 1971, I graduated from St. Thomas grammar school. Then I was off to the next phase of my Catholic education, Bishop Fenwick High School. It was conveniently located just half a mile down the street from my grammar school. My best friend's mother would pick me up in front of the church steps, every morning around 7:45 A.M. and drive us to school. My brother Junior was attending a private High School in Danvers at the same time. From 1969–1979, Doris had two children in private schools or college during any given year.

I was so excited and nervous because I was going to start high school. The only good thing about this school was that they had done away with the school uniforms the prior year. No more plaid skirts, neckties and knee socks for me. Doris wasn't that happy because it meant I actually needed a wardrobe. School shopping would entail more than new underwear, shoes and a few new white blouses.

By the 70s, the number of nuns was dwindling and 50% of the faculty at the school were laymen and women. Since lay teachers actually had to be paid and hadn't taken a vow of poverty, the school had to limit the courses due to financial restraints. No longer were life courses like cooking and sewing offered. So the principal, Mr. Lapointe, felt if he could get some of the parents to volunteer to teach, he could set up a "mini course" program. Students could take six-week courses for 60 minutes a week in such subjects as cooking, sewing and car repair.

Once again the flyer came home explaining the plan, and Doris was the first one to send it back and volunteer to teach cooking. Her classroom would be the teacher's lounge because it had a three-burner electric stove, oven and a lot of counter space for prepping. The class was scheduled at 1 P.M. on Wednesdays, the perfect time to cook a meal and eat it. Doris was working full time and got her boss to allow her to take a two-hour lunch on Wednesday and work later at the end of the day.

Doris took this course very seriously and wanted her eight students to learn the most they could in six short weeks. She created a syllabus with each week's meal plan and handed it out the first week.

Week 1: Basic bread dough
Week 2: Macaroni and cheese
Week 3: Fried boneless chicken
Week 4: Meat loaf
Week 5: Tomato sauce and meatballs
Week 6: Creating a lasagna

The first week started with your basic bread dough. By teaching them the principles of flour, water, yeast and kneading techniques, they would be able to make any bread recipe. There was her basic fried dough or fancy twisted breads for holidays. Doris had a system; bring a completed meal to actually serve and then the ingredients for the students to recreate it. The meal that was made during class was given to the few remaining sisters to take to the convent to bake or fry for their supper. By doing it this way, the nuns were guaranteed five meals when Doris was finished.

The first day of class, Doris brought a bowl of perfect bread dough that was already raised and ready to fry, to make into rolls, or to create a loaf of bread. The girls all had their own ingredients and under Doris' tutelage, they got down and dirty. Doris taught the correct way to test your yeast by mixing it in warm water and sugar. Only if the yeast doubled in size would it be used, if it didn't, it would be thrown away and restart the process. My mother was a big fan of Fleishman's dry yeast, and that's all she would use. Next, the flour and kneading, again only using King Arthur's, unbleached white flour into any of her bread products.

Once they had created their dough, it was put aside to rise. The girls fried Doris' prepared dough, formed perfect dinner rolls and twisted bread that was then baked. From the first day, word spread that on Wednesday's at 2:15 P.M. there would be culinary treats in the teacher's lounge. All of a sudden, Doris' class was the happening place. All of the teachers, nuns and the Chaplin were descending upon the lounge, all under the pretense of being friendly and wanting to meet Mrs. Brown. In reality they were after the food.

In Doris' haste to clean up all the dough and flour and get back to work, she had forgotten about the rising dough. It was in the corner of the lounge being kept warm and hidden from view under a dark plaid, wool blanket. There were eight bowls and each held 2 cups of flour and one packet of yeast. The world had not started its crusade about fuel conservation, so the school heat was kept at 70 degrees at all times.

The following morning, the first teacher to arrive to school went to make the pot of coffee in the teacher's lounge. When she got to the room, she thought she heard a plopping sound coming from behind the door. She was a little concerned about whom or what was making that strange sound. She called out and there was no answer. What could it be? Slowly, she turned the handle on the door and began to peek in. What she saw could only be described as a scene from the horror movie *The Blob*. All of the white, warm, sticky bread dough had risen all night out of their ceramic bowls, slithered down the counter and across the gray speckled tile floor. It was alive!

When the other teachers arrived, they couldn't believe what they saw. They were all convinced that the dough was actually trying to escape from the room. The eight cooking students were called down to the lounge and clean up began. Mr. Lapointe notified Doris of the incident. She was all apologetic, and he assured her it was okay and try to be more careful in the future. What else was he to do? He couldn't fire a volunteer.

For the following four weeks, Doris was on her best behavior. She had become the favorite new teacher of her eight students due to her easygoing, comical teaching style. Doris had followed her syllabus to the letter. The previous week, the class had created a batch of meatballs and tomato sauce that Doris had taken home and froze. Her intention was to thaw it and bring it back on week six, and have the girls create their first Italian Lasagna.

Doris arrived a little early so she could get the sauce warming up on the stove. Once the students arrived they began. A large pot of salted, cold water, with 2 tablespoons of olive oil, was placed on the burner and brought to a boil. It was a rule to start with fresh cold water because you didn't want hot water that had been sitting in the hot water heater. It took a little longer, but my mother was convinced that the pasta tasted better.

While things were heating up, she whipped the one pound of fresh, creamy ricotta cheese in a bowl with one egg and half cup of grated Parmesan cheese. She took the yellow ball of whole mozzarella cheese, cut into quarter inch cubes. Last, she sliced the tender juicy meatball about a quarter inch thick and waited. Once the lasagna noodles had been cooked, according to the package directions, and drained, it was time for the assembly line. Doris was very specific about cooking all pasta before using it in a recipe. On one occasion when teaching the 19-year-old newlywed across the street to make macaroni and cheese, the poor girl had poured the cheese sauce over dry, from-the-box elbows. Doris swore she would never assume that people knew what to do. She would go with the philosophy that they didn't have a clue and start from scratch.

Doris lined the young ladies up along the table and each one had a station: tomato sauce, ricotta, mozzarella, Parmesan, meatballs, and noodles. One girl had the all-important job of carrying the pan and following the layering sequence that Doris recited.

— Tomato sauce, coat bottom of pan lightly
— Layer of noodles, neatly lined up with no spaces between them
— Spoon large amounts of the whipped ricotta evenly onto the noodles
— Cover with second layer of noodles, press down gently
— Tomato sauce to cover completely approximately a quarter inch thick
— Evenly disperse the mozzarella cubes all over the sauce covered noodles
— Sprinkle with grated parmesan
— Cover with third layer of noodles
— Tomato sauce, quarter inch thick

— Gently place the meatball slices along the noodles
— Cover with final layer on noodles
— Coat noodles with thin coating of sauce to prevent drying
— Bake at 350 degrees for approximately one hour
— Remove from oven and let rest for 15 minutes for ricotta
    to stiffen
— Serve and Eat

Like magic, Doris removed perfect, bubbling lasagna from the oven and put the students one into bake. Usually, she would let the tray sit on the stove for 15 minutes to let the ricotta set, but there wasn't time, so she started to serve.

All the regulars were there for the grand finale of her successful class. Everyone was complimenting Doris, and she immediately gave all the praise to her students. She told them how much she had enjoyed sharing her passion with them by teaching them to cook.

Everyone was just completing their lunch when a newcomer entered the room. What was that dirty smudge on his forehead? Did I mention that Doris' class was on Wednesdays? Father Dominic almost chocked on the bite that he was chewing. Doris could not have served a room full of priests and Catholics, meat on Ash Wednesday, could she? The answer was yes. For the non-Catholics, this is a big holy day that begins the season of Lent. It was one of the very few holy days that a person had to abstain from eating all meat products. The only exemption was for medical reasons.

Doris was speechless. What had she done? It was an honest mistake. She had been so busy preparing for the finale class that she didn't get to church at 7 A.M., and get her ashes. Her plan had been to go to class, finish up at work and catch the 5 P.M. mass. Father Dominic could see how upset she was. Everyone was confident that if Doris had remembered it was Ash Wednesday, before noon, she would have skipped the meat layer. My mother's ability to get into these situations has always amazed me. Doris never had anything but good intentions and was always 100% sincere, yet it still happened.

Not to worry, Doris was not excommunicated that day. Father Dominic was an older, wiser priest and as guilty as everyone else. He bestowed upon every person in the room absolution. It didn't matter whether you had eaten the lasagna or not. Just say two Hail Marys and two Our Fathers, and you would be forgiven.

Unfortunately, the mini course project only lasted that one semester. They had such a small parent response that they were not able to offer enough courses to make it worthwhile. I never believed the rumors it was canceled because they couldn't have any more incidents, involving their clergy reported to the archdiocese.

Plimouth Plantation Chaperone

The sisters at St. Thomas only had to say, "Mrs. Brown, can you?" and before the entire request had been uttered, Doris would have said yes. Most of the time, she would say yes blindly. Doris felt she was never too busy to do anything the sisters wanted or needed. This time the request was to chaperone Sister Agnes fourth grade class that I was a part of.

We were going to the Plimouth Plantation located in historic Plymouth, Massachusetts. Plymouth was south of Peabody, closer to Cape Cod. It was 64 miles away, but in 1967 you had to go straight through downtown Boston, during the morning commute. Plymouth was where our forefathers came and settled on November 11, 1620 upon the famous ship the Mayflower. Here the Puritans set up the first settlement in Massachusetts; home of the world renowned Plymouth Rock. It was believed to be where the first foot was placed on land in the new world. I always thought it was this enormous bolder, but when I first saw it I couldn't help but laugh. It was a rock about 5 feet wide, 3 feet long and 4 feet tall and sits on land in the middle of a small park. It was surrounded by an iron railing to keep anyone else from ever stepping on it again.

The yellow school bus had arrived and was parked less than 20 feet outside the all-purpose room at the back of the St. Thomas grammar school. This was important because the day was grey and dismal, and it vacillated between periods of drizzle to torrential downpours. All I could think was this trip could be a washout.

The 52 students neatly lined up along the auditorium wall in single file. My class was standing along a bank of windows and could see the weather conditions and were already starting to whine. The comments were: "We can't go in the rain, we will get all wet." "It won't be any fun." "We don't want to go anymore." Doris, two other mothers and Sister Agnes were not going to give up the faith. Not to mention the trip was paid for, and there was no refund.

Sister Agnes was encouraging the children to say a little prayer to Jesus to ask him to send some better weather for our trip. Mrs. Jones was being sickly sweet with her soft-spoken melodic voice, "Don't you worry children, everything will turn out just fine. You will see." Doris' approach was more direct, like a drill sergeant, "The bus is here, the trip is paid for, so we're going. Everyone on the bus now! Stop the whining, it will be fine once we get on the road."

The road Doris had referred to was over the Tobin/Mystic River Bridge and through downtown Boston. We could look down from the bus as commuters honked horns and yelled an occasional verbal obscenity or waved an improper gesture. Bostonians have never had the most courteous driving reputation, and it has only gotten worse over the years. What should have been a 50–60 minute trip according to the Map Quest technology of 2009, took us that long just to exit downtown Boston and get on the Mass Turnpike.

Doris could sense the natives were getting restless. They were all asking the proverbial question "Are we there yet?" She had gone to Plymouth many times in her life since one of her favorite cousins had lived there. Being trapped on the bus, knowing there was at least an hour remaining, Doris made a decision and announced, "Let's all sing."

The only thing that Doris Brown could not do was sing. Her voice was loud, off key and she could never remember the words and would start humming instead. We started with the Girl Scout standard Kum Bah Ya. The lyrics were easy, and it had the appropriate Lord references. The only problem was that after 30 to 40 repetitions, it loses its charm.

It was obvious that the boys didn't appreciate this sissy song, so we began the ever-popular "100 Bottles of Beer on the Wall." The topic might have been a little shaky for a bus full of Catholic school kids, but it did have an educational benefit: learning to count backwards. Sister Agnes was more worried about the weather outside her window than Doris' song selection.

The last bottle of beer had finally fallen off of the wall, and we were out of Boston and heading out into the suburbs. In 1967, the land had not been totally developed into cookie-cutter housing developments of six room ranches or capes. The landscape was still very rural with vegetable and dairy farms. There were rolling hills and miles of grassy fields dotted with cows.

The children were losing their faith and Sister Agnes had just the strategy. If Jesus isn't hearing our prayers, maybe there is a lot of prayer volume today due to the inclement weather, so pray to the Blessed Mother Mary instead. Everyone knew that Jesus could never deny his mother any request, so her plan was to sneak in the backdoor to the big guy. This is when I think Doris realized we might truly be in trouble.

As we drove farther south, I was fascinated at the number of cows we encountered. I had always been under the impression that cows, milk, cheese, and my favorite, ice cream were associated with Vermont, not Massachusetts. Suddenly, Doris started clapping her hands to get everyone's attention. In her boisterous voice, she started yelling, "Let me have your attention. Quiet, please. Let me have your attention." All of a sudden, I became queasy. What was she going to do next?

Doris ran up and down the bus aisle the whole time pointing out of the starboard side of the bus yelling, "What are they doing? What are they doing?" Who, or should I ask what was she referring to? There was dead silence. I think that people felt the wrong answer could put her over the edge of sanity. From somewhere in the back of the bus, this little squeaky voice uttered, "They're standing in the rain." Was that the answer she wanted? I just sat on the edge of my seat and waited.

What happened next shocked me as well as Sister Agnes. Doris threw her hands into the air like one of those Bible-belt evangelists and said, "My son, you are 100% correct." I was still confused. My 10-year-old brain could not follow my mother's thought process. I thought, 100% correct about what? What was she talking about?

There was an eerie pause, and she once again started walking up and down the bus aisle. Then she said it, "The cows are standing up. They are not sitting. They are not lying down. The cows are all standing in the rain." Okay, at least she had clued us in on whom, but the why still didn't make any sense. Then she was off again, pointing her finger at random children and asking, "Do you know what that means, do you?"

This time there was no brave volunteer to answer her. My classmates were afraid even any movement would start her ranting again. I glanced over at Sister Agnes for some reassurance, only she was pale and her mouth was hanging open. Had Doris finally lost her sanity? She walked to the center of the bus, scanned the 52 silent children and in a loud, clear calm manner said the answer we were all dying to hear. "It means no rain. Everyone knows that if the cows are standing up, it isn't going to rain." Was this a trick question? Yes, she was correct, the cows were definitely standing, but they were already standing in the pouring rain.

Everyone on the bus had been so preoccupied with the Doris drama that was unfolding that we failed to see the sign, Plimouth Plantation, until we entered the parking lot. Call it what you want, divine intervention, a miracle, or God just felt Doris couldn't handle another drop of rain. The once-dark bus was suddenly filled with bright sunshine from that glowing ball of incandescent gases in the sky. The clouds had parted, revealing a blue sky and a perfect summer day.

To say that the entire group was stunned for a few seconds would have been an understatement. Then the bus erupted into cheers. My classmates went wild with excitement. Doris had been right all along. I think Sister Agnes' faith was tested that day, not her belief in God, but in the power of Doris. We were filing off the bus when I passed my mother and she whispered, "Ye of little faith."

Doris had and still does have a deep faith in God. Following her divorce and remarriage in 1982, she stopped going to church. Her feeling was, if the church was going to excommunicate her for finally being happy with her new husband, why go? The Catholic Church allowed her to attend Mass and they were happy to take her money, only no Sacrament of Holy communion. Doris was never a hypocrite and why should she attend a club that charged dues and only allowed her limited benefits? Doris always prayed at home and felt she and God could do their talking in her own living room. She didn't need a brick building.

Today Doris actually spends two to three hours a day in actual prayer. She chooses the Rosary as her bead of choice and prayers from the St. Jude society. Throughout her life, if someone were ill or had a life altering decision to make, Doris would pray for him or her. I once asked her to pray that I would get another job that paid well and her answer was, "I'll pray that God gives you the job you need, but never pray for money."

Doris The World Traveler

When Doris got into her forties, she got a new unlisted telephone number and the last digits were 36-42. To be able to remember it she started saying, "I would rather be 36, but I'm going to be 42." Fortunately for her, she was actually going to be 42 a few months later, which gave her time to learn her new telephone number. The realization that she was already 40-plus and had just given birth to her second child caused a mini mid-life crisis. Being a big believer in sayings, such as "Life begins at forty," she set out to make it true.

Doris really hadn't traveled to many places. Her childhood was spent in Peabody, and visits to relatives in Plymouth, Massachusetts and Providence, Rhode Island by car. The first and only time she had been on a plane was the flight to Toronto to arrange her cousin Alicia's husband's funeral. Doris does mention that she sat next to the famous Duke Ellington on the flight home, only he wasn't very talkative. I wish I had been a fly on the plane to witness that exchange. I bet Mr. Ellington was never the same after meeting my mother. Her honeymoon was spent at resort in New Hampshire, the Allen A in 1949. This was probably the first and last true vacation Doris had ever had.

It was the late 1960s and family travel was becoming more popular. Teenagers were taking summer vacations to Europe, backpacking through 21 countries in 14 days. We were already spending summers at our travel trailer in Wells, Maine, only Doris was restless; she wanted more. Doris devised a grand plan to take a two week vacation biyearly and see more of the world or at least continental North America.

O'Canada

Doris decided to plan a trip for the following summer. A fellow camper told her about a beautiful place called the Bay of Fundy in New Brunswick, Canada. At that time, I don't believe Doris even knew where that was. Geography was not one of her strong subjects in high school.

The woman had described rock formations 100 feet tall that looked like planters that had pine trees growing out of the tops. The tide supposedly came in with one giant swoosh so everyone had to be off the beach or they would be pulled out to sea. Doris' method of researching a vacation destination was to rely on word of mouth and testimonials from fellow campers that she knew and trusted.

Doris knew this was the biggest vacation she had ever attempted to plan, so she called Triple AAA Auto Service and joined. It meant a free Trip Kit for her vacation destinations, and it didn't hurt to have the roadside service if the poor green Rambler broke down while we were away. They would provide an old-fashioned, foldable paper map and it would be highlighted for the easiest route to take. No estimates of times or distances were involved. My father still had a friend in the Camper group, the 49'ers, that he consulted. Harry gave him a campground directory for Maine and eastern Canada and suggestions on where to stay. It had all the makings of a National Lampoon movie, The Canadian Vacation, only substitute the Browns for the Griswolds.

In July, the Browns, affectionately referred to as the Beverly Hillbillies by our close friends and neighbors, started our summer vacation. Doris did have enough sense to realize that the old Rambler could not pull the weight of the 17-foot travel trailer we owned. Plan B was the next best thing: rent a tent trailer. It weighed less, set up easily, and had the luxury of real beds with mattresses and a small kitchenette inside. The trailer rental salesman assured her the six-cylinder, seven-year-old Rambler could handle the towing with no problem. I wish someone had asked the poor green Rambler if it felt it could handle it.

I would have never used the words quiet, patient and mechanically competent to describe my father. A more accurate description would have been loud, quick-tempered and mechanically challenged. There he was trying to remember how to attach a trailer to the ball hitch on the back of our car. He did remember that there was something that got plugged in to activate the directionals and brake lights on the back of the trailer. The safety chains that were required to make sure that the trailer stayed attached to the car at all times proved to be a little more challenging. Thank God my 13-year-old brother was there taking it all in. Junior could build or fix anything and he didn't even need the written directions. It was always a mystery that they were born on the same date, and yet they were as far apart as two people can be. It must have something to do with the theory of "nature verses nurture."

Step 1 was completed when the trailer was finally hooked up to the car. Next came the essential directions on setting up once we got to our destination. Dad received a quick five-minute lesson on backing up with a trailer since there were no drive-through campsites where we could stop for the night. It seemed a little tricky to me, but I was only 10 years old at the time. Last, he learned how to pop it up, slide out the beds, and put the braces in place to prevent the whole camper from toppling over once we laid down for the night. I really don't think Doris ever took into consideration the part my father had in making our vacations a success or a failure. Sometimes, looking back, I wish she had.

After what felt like days, we were all loaded into the car, Junior in shotgun (front passenger seat), since he was the only one with any sense of direction. If we had any hope of getting to Canada, it was all up to my brother and that trip kit. Try and imagine 3 people in a small backseat, a car radio with maybe three stations and none of them F.M. We didn't even have any type of tape player, cassette or 8 track to use when we lost radio signal. Technology was still a dream that hadn't even been dreamt. I look back and I think my daughters would die today if they were in a car and didn't have their MP3 players or an old CD player if they had to. It brings into perspective how much has changed in the past 40 years in the areas of technology, electronics and computers.

Day one, and it seemed like we never got out of Maine because we didn't. The names of all the cities along the Maine coastline, like Belfast, Sweden and Stockholm, made it seem as though we were traveling through Europe. We spent night one in a nice campground, and the men did a great job of setting up. Doris splurged an extra dollar to have electric and water hook ups on our site so she wouldn't have to light lanterns during the night. My mother liked the concept of camping because it was a reasonably priced way to travel; I don't think it was the being in the woods that she relished.

On the morning of day two, we got an early start. Cold cereal and milk for breakfast was considered a delicacy for us. Doris thought the cold-boxed cereals were too expensive to have on a daily basis, so we only received them out of convenience on vacation. We each got to choose one cereal to take on the trip. My brothers were always predictable: Junior was always Captain Crunch, because it always came with some pirate toy. Toney loved Lucky Charms because they are magically delicious. I, on the other hand, had a dilemma as to which one to choose. To me, sugar was a good thing and the more the better. So would it be Sugar Frosted Flakes or Sugar Snaps? On this trip, I had to flip a coin and the Sugar Frosted Flakes won out. It's funny that later in life when white sugar became the enemy of the people, all the same cereals removed the word sugar from their names. It was assumed that at the same time they also removed a percentage of sugar from their product. On the rare occasion that I have had my beloved Frosted Flakes in the past 30+ years, they still taste the same to me, "They're Great."

The Browns were back into the car and on the road again. This day, the natives were restless and we still had six hours to go. We had lost radio signal long before we crossed over the border into Canada. All we heard was the noise of the car tires on the asphalt. Doris said, "Let's all sing." I thought, okay, I can do that for a while. I wish Doris had taken the time to learn some new songs because she started with her favorite "Kum Ba Ya." I think we did maybe three rounds and my brother refused to sing anymore. He decided he wanted the "100 Bottles of Beer on the Wall" song. I was starting to sound hoarse at beer 45 when I looked over at Dad. The veins in his neck were beginning to bulge and his face was beet red. I thought the top of his head was going to blow off. Was he mad or was he having a stroke?

My father had been the only one actually watching the road. That was a good thing since he was the one driving the car. What we had missed was the breath-taking scenery along the coastline. The road was so narrow that the jagged cliffs were only a few feet away from the car. Only it wasn't the coast that had him nervous, it was the mountain range we had just entered. The road seemed to go straight up to the blue sky. There were two lanes on the inclines, and slower traffic was to stay to the right. I feared for our poor little lime green Rambler, because even in the slow lane trailer trucks sped passed her. It was even worse on the down slope. There was an enormous sign warning about the steep grade and to slow down. I started to feel his anxiety when I read another sign about what to do if your brakes failed. I started to pray that a mechanic had checked out the car and brakes prior to the trip. My father didn't have a clue what preventative car maintenance meant. I recalled when he realized it might be a good idea to change the oil once and awhile and it was so old, it drained out like molasses.

Doris had another way to handle her obvious anxiety: she used humor. The next song she sang was "The Little Engine That Could." I had been under the impression that title was a storybook, but my mother was improvising. Every time a mountain appeared Doris would sing, "Chug a chug chug. Chug a chug chug. I think I can, I think I can." After we had made it up the mountain safely and were heading down the back, she would do her Gomer Pyle imitation from the Andy Griffith show and yell, "Surprise, surprise, surprise." I don't think my dad ever appreciated Doris' sense of humor. He wasn't laughing that day.

We finally made it to The Bay of Fundy. As we were pulling into a lovely camp ground only minutes from the beach, our poor car blew something. There was steam coming out from under her hood, and all her water and antifreeze had leaked onto the ground. Thank God for the Triple AAA Auto Service. We called the only mechanic in the area and he had the car towed to his station. Bad news was that he didn't have the part, a water pump, in stock. If he waited for it to be shipped from Edmundton, it would mean days without a car. There was another solution: the man in the next campsite was willing to drive my father the 90 minutes each way to the auto part store. Dad could have the water pump back and replaced the same day. Campers were and still are a very nice, loyal group of people. I'm sure his generous offer had nothing to do with the fact that his family was going horseback riding that day and he didn't seem to be the animal lover type.

While he was gone, we walked to the beach and were able to swim, even though the water was quite chilly, around 62 degrees. The reddish brown clay rock formations seemed to grow right out of the beach. They were not really flowerpot-shaped, but looked more like a vase, and the blue-green pine trees were the flowers protruding out. We did get to witness the phenomena of the tide coming in all at once. A loud horn went off and everyone cleared the beach. We watched the swirling surf way out, and then two waves later it was at the rock wall. I'm not sure if the current was strong enough or there was a rip tide that could have dragged you out to sea, but the water depth went from one-inch deep to 10 feet deep in minutes. Since Doris couldn't swim, it could have definitely have dragged her out to sea.

Our neighbors had so much fun on their horseback riding outing that Doris surprised us the next day. She informed us over breakfast "We are going horseback riding today!" We would be able to experience the views along the seaside trails and be closer to nature. Dad did not seem to embrace this idea or any plan that involved animals of any kind. He was very happy to learn that Toney was too small, so he had to take him to the beach instead.

The stable was within walking distance, so being without the car for that day was not an inconvenience. It was going to be delivered later that day, good as new. The stable was a two-story barn, all gray and weathered, with red shutters. The double front doors were wide open, and the staff was leading out the potential horses that we would ride.

There appeared to be about 12 riders, mostly women and teenage girls. My brother was the only male and one of the tallest riders at around 5 feet 9 inches. It was like watching a horse show. The horses were led out one at a time, paraded in front of the group, and then tied to the ranch fence. I fell in love with a slightly rotund black and gray mare named Daisy, who had a white circle over her right eye.

Out of nowhere came a chestnut stallion at least 16 hands tall and he was whining and bucking the entire time. No one was surprised to hear his name was, appropriately, Diablo. Suddenly, Junior went white as a sheet. He came to the realization that horses were matched to the rider, and he was the tallest and the only male. He ran to our mother and said, "Mom, I don't want to ride. Please don't make me ride?" Doris replied, "Sorry Junior, it's too late, five bucks too late." There was a no-refund sign and Doris had paid the $5 for the adults, and $2.50 for me, half price for a child ticket, since I was still under 12.

It was time to saddle up, and it took three stable hands to get poor Junior into the saddle. Doris was seated on a very slow, gray mare named Bessie, just her speed. The horses were so programmed to do the tour that they fell into a single line without much prodding. Doris' horse kept attempting to go into the woods and eat grass. It didn't matter how hard she pulled on the reins or gave Bessie a little kick, this horse was determined to eat, not walk. Finally, she was led to the head of the line by one of the stable hands and we were off.

The ride was advertised as an exciting, two-hour scenic adventure on horseback. Exciting being the key word, only I think leisurely might have been more descriptive. A 90-year-old could have come as long as they could keep their body in an upright sitting position for the two hours. Most of the time, I really didn't need to hold the reins; my Daisy never moved more than one or two paces without actually taking a pause. The advertisement was truthful about the scenery. It was spectacular.

The excursion was almost complete when the horse behind Diablo decided to create some trouble and bit him on his hindquarters. There was this high-pitched whinny behind me, and when I turned, I saw Diablo up on his hind legs and Junior holding on for dear life. He grabbed the reins, saddle horn and a large handful of mane and was able to stay seated. The staff was very efficient and my brother was off the horse and standing on the ground within minutes. Physically, Junior was unharmed, but emotionally he was shaking. I know for a fact that today at 50 plus years old, Junior has never sat on another horse. He tells Doris that she scarred him for life because it was $5 too late.

We managed to complete our vacation without any more mishaps. My father got an alternative route for the return trip and it went more inland with fewer mountains. It proved to be the last hurrah for the lime green Rambler, and she had given it her all. Doris was so proud of her idea and began immediately planning the next vacation 2 years from July. It would prove to be a biyearly event for at least a decade.

The Cheap Motel

Where had the time gone? It was two years later and the Browns' 2nd biannual summer vacation was about to begin. Doris was so pleased with Canada and New Brunswick that she decided to stay in Canada, only this time we headed west. We started in Quebec and continued to Montreal and back down through Vermont and home. Doris had more time for research and had read about the 1967 Worlds Fair in Montreal. Why not go there on the way back? The fact that it was 1970 meant the fees should be cheaper and the facility less crowded.

Unfortunately, the family's trusted lime green Rambler had died and gone to the big junkyard in the sky six months prior. I still fondly remember its cracked vinyl seats and push-button transmission. To this day, I don't think they ever came up with that lime green paint color again. She had been a classic.

We were now the proud owners of a used 1968 maroon Ford station wagon. It had been purchased from a neighbor during the divorce settlement. It was the most sophisticated car I had ever seen. Leather seats, A.M./F.M. stereo radio with the new sensation, 8-track cassette, and a third rear-facing seat. Unfortunately, it was not equipped with a ball hitch to tow the trailer, which was just fine with Dad because after his last ordeal, he outright refused to ever tow anything again. We really could not blame him.

Doris was never one to run away from a problem or a challenge, and this was not any different. The plan was the same; two-week vacation, inexpensive lodging, Canada, and have fun. Camping was still the number one option for reasonably priced accommodations. No law said it had to be a trailer or a tent trailer. What was wrong with a good old-fashioned tent? It would be a less expensive option since we could borrow everything and save the rental fees, which in turn meant more luxuries, like meals out and organized tours.

It was decided that we would tent and everything was on track again. Once again, Doris did not think through all the possible scenarios, such as a flat tire with the back of the car filled to capacity, making it impossible to get to the spare. No problem, we still had the dependable Triple AAA. The uncomfortable cots guaranteed that there would not be a good night's sleep for 14 days. Last and most important, what was the contingency plan if we got rain, I mean real, fat old rain, say for days and days? So I did convince her to have a slush fund available for possible cheap, inexpensive, clean motel rooms.

Doris called around to friends and fellow campers to begin Operation Camping Equipment. I gave her credit, she was able to borrow a two-room tent that slept six; a camp stove; and two Coleman oil lanterns. The remainder of the gear; such as coolers, pots and pans, and dishes, we had from our own trailer. The Browns loaded up with the handy trip kit map safely in Junior's hands, and we were "On the Road Again." I doubt Willie Nelson knew that we had used his song title 20 years prior.

This time it was like driving in a Cadillac in comparison to the poor Rambler. It was spacious, and the music from the stereo was wonderful. Even after we lost radio signal, we still had the 8 tracks. I do admit, as children, we didn't have the cassette selection that my daughters have today. Anything was an improvement over nothing to listen to. We had threatened Doris' life that there was to be no singing, especially her rendition of "Kum Ba Ya." I was willing to listen to anything, even my mother's three 8 track tapes: The Mills Brothers, Dean Martin and Tony Bennett. It was sad because at 13 years old, I knew all the words to "Cab Driver," "Amore," and "I left My Heart In San Franscio." It was not something I would admit to anyone or was proud of at the time.

The travel route that had been planned by Triple AAA took us through Vermont, north to Quebec. No more hours on end going through the backwoods towns of Maine. The trip seemed to go a lot smoother. Maybe it was the fact that there was no appendage at the back of our car and Dad seemed much calmer, which translated into the whole family being much calmer. Plus, we were all two years older and more mature. I don't remember as much whining or fighting in the car.

Suddenly, our luck was about to change. We were already in Canada, only hours from our destination, when it started to rain. The wipers could not keep up with the sheets of water attacking the windshield. There were a few occasions when the visibility was zero and Dad had to pull over to the side of the road. Doris kept saying not to worry, it was going to clear up ahead and when we got to the campground everything would be fine. I wasn't sure what she based her weather forecast on since we hadn't seen a cow in five hours.

This time, Doris' weather forecast was incorrect. It was starting to get dark and even she had to admit that we would not be able to pitch a tent in this heavy rain. Doris made a supreme decision to find an inexpensive motel for the night. We had planned our sleepovers based on the campground directory, so we had no clue about motels in the area. Then, through the rain, we made out a sign for what looked like a motel or hotel up ahead.

Since we were in a French province, it made quick reading of the road signs difficult. Junior had already taken two years of French in high school and was more fluent in speaking than reading. Doris, on the other hand, could read and write in Portuguese and kept saying the words looked familiar. Only Doris could look at a sign in French, interpret it into Portuguese and translate its meaning back into English. This should have been a clue that we were in for trouble.

We had taken the exit and were seeing flashing lights ahead and a building that looked like it could be a motel. We yelled at Dad to pull into the parking lot so we could slowly survey the situation. There was a beautiful Victorian home with a wide staircase that led up to a farmer's porch. Like arms from a torso were a row of motel rooms from each end of the porch. The motel section had no style: it was clapboard shingles painted white and the doors were red and numbered. There seemed to be a corresponding car or truck parked in front of each door. There was a moment of panic in the car. Was the motel full? The sign out front did not say "No Vacancy."

Doris said, "There is only way to find out. Junior, let's go in and ask." Since my brother was the closest thing we had to someone who actually spoke French, in case no one inside spoke English, he was the logical choice to accompany our mother. Prior to our trip, Junior took it upon himself to learn some key phrases in French that were not in his curriculum. How much? Do you take a charge card? Where is the bathroom? Dad pulled our station wagon in front of the wide staircase at the main house, where the sign read Office, and the two of them were off and literally running.

They entered through the front door into a foyer, and straight ahead was a large counter-high desk, made out of solid cherry. A middle-aged, slightly plump woman with curly graying hair manned the desk. Behind her to the left, was a massive staircase that curved up to the second floor. All the woodwork was solid cherry and very ornate with various moldings and trims.

To either side of the hall were rooms that ran the length of the first floor. The room on the right appeared to be a dining room with five small, mismatched tables and a massive marble fireplace on the far wall. Over the fireplace was a mirror, trimmed in an ornate gold leaf frame. The room on the left was a formal parlor with two Queen Anne sofas done in crushed red velvet. They were flanked on either side with delicate gold metal tables. Doris began to panic; we couldn't afford to stay at a hotel as beautiful as this.

They walked up to the woman and Junior asked her in French, "Parle' vous English?" she replied, "A little." Not wasting any time, Doris asked, "How much for a room?" The woman kept looking at them with a quizzical look and said $2 American. Doris was in disbelief. How could it be so cheap? Before the woman could rethink the price, Doris handed her the money and took the key. We were given a room on the second floor of the main house. Doris felt there could be a problem with the room since it was so inexpensive, so she decided to check it out before she dragged the entire family and luggage in.

Doris was amazed as to how many rooms there were down the long corridor. The room was number 6 and was only a few doors down from the stairs. As they got to the door, Doris noticed an official state seal over the door jam. It was some Board of Health inspection with the seal of approval. Doris opened the door using an old-fashioned brass key that fit into an old keyhole-type lock. The room was very plain, with light yellow walls and white sheers at the windows. The furnishings were sparse two double beds with padded Hollywood-style headboards, thin white popcorn chenille bedspreads, a wooden chair in the corner and a small dresser. Doris pulled down the bed clothing and found the sheets clean and fresh smelling. The room had also passed Doris' seal of approval.

It was time to get the rest of the family and luggage from the car and get a good night's sleep. When my mother and Junior went back down the stairs, the woman wasn't at the desk. On the return trip, Toney, Junior, Dad, Doris and I came through the door into the lobby, and the woman was once again at her post behind the desk. She just stood there with her mouth wide open. It was as though she could not believe what she was looking at. Doris just said, "See you tomorrow morning." There was no response from our hostess, she just stood dazed.

Doris set up the sleeping arrangements, and once again I got the cot and sleeping bag while everyone else got a real bed. Being the only girl, I always seemed to get the lesser of the sleeping accommodations. If it was a tent I had the cot and my family had airbeds. The upgraded tent trailer, I got the narrow air mattress to their full size beds. In a motel I could have had a comfortable fold away bed but that meant an extra dollar, so it was the army cot from the car. It really was a moot point because all I remembered was my head hitting the pillow and I was asleep. I apparently had slept through all the excitement.

When I woke the next morning around 6:30, Doris was sitting on the lone wooden chair in the corner. The boys were still asleep, all tucked into their bed. Something was wrong, Doris looked terrible. I asked, "Mom, are you alright? Are you sick? You look exhausted." My mother had dark circles under her eyes that didn't stop until they crested on her cheekbones. Her hair was flattened at the back of her head where she had apparently had it resting against the wall all night. "Did you sit up all night?" I asked.

Apparently after I had fallen asleep, the motel started to rock. The dining room and parlor on the first floor had a live band with loud music until at least 2:00 A.M. That wasn't so bad, but after the music all the guests seemed to come to the second floor and the noise was worse. There were beds hitting the walls, doors opening and slamming shut. Doris had never heard such moaning and groaning noises before in her naive life.

It was all starting to make sense to Doris. The woman's slightly confused look when Doris came in to register with a 15-year-old boy. The shocked look when the whole family ascended the stairs to the second floor. We had just spent the night in a French Whore house. We had stayed in a brothel, a house of ill repute. Not to worry, the Government Seal of Approval over the door assured us that the ladies were all free of communicable diseases. Apparently, this house had two options: you could bring your own date or choose from the house staff. It now made complete sense to Doris why the price of the room was so reasonable. It must have been the hourly rate and she just misunderstood.

Everyone was waking up, so Doris decided to make the best out of a bad situation and we all showered and went downstairs to check out. There was the same woman from the night before at the bottom of the staircase. Doris walked up to her and said, "You played a dirty trick on me." The woman smiled at my mother and in broken English apologized. She had been in shock when she saw the entire family go up the stairs and she didn't know what to do. The inclement weather was persistent and it was 50 miles to the nearest hotel. To make up for what she had done, she offered to make us all a big breakfast on the house. Doris could see that the woman was being sincere, so we all went into the lovely dining room and sat down for breakfast.

My mother sat at a separate table with the madam, and she proceeded to tell my mother her life story. She had four young children when her husband had been killed in a car accident. Her formal education was limited, and she needed a way to support her family and be able to be at home with them. So she took the insurance money and invested it in the oldest business in the world, prostitution. The motel sections had been added later as business was growing. The woman made a point of telling Doris that she was the boss and was not involved in the entertainment end. In Quebec, prostitution was a legal business and the government, for a piece of the action, supervised it all.

Since it was Sunday and we were good Catholics, Doris asked "Is there a Catholic church close by?" Doris felt that a few extra payers couldn't hurt after last night. The fact that it was only day two of our long, 14-day vacation, she figured some extra protection was warranted. We were in luck; the church was five miles away, straight ahead on Main St. The Madam told us to leave our bags and pack up after or we would miss the last mass of the day.

We easily located the church since it was a massive red brick structure with a steeple 100 feet in the sky. On entering St. Therese's, you were mesmerized by the stained glass windows. The sun shone through them sending multicolored sparkles across the walls. The pews were styled like the old protestant churches, with high backs and small wooden hinged doors to close off the pews once the family had arrived.

Doris gave the church a quick survey to spot any empty pews that would fit our family of five. Since we were really not dressed as well as the members, she tried to stay toward the back. On the right was an empty pew and we all slid in and knelt down to pray. Within a few minutes, a man was standing at the door and motioning us to move. He was whispering in French that we were in his family's pew and had to leave. We moved back two rows only to have the same thing happen. What ever happened to the idea that anyone can enter God's house and worship?

I felt as though everyone was staring at the stupid Americans. Then an elderly woman with white hair and big ruby cheeks took pity on us. She walked up the aisle and gently grabbed my mother's arm and motioned to the way back where she was sitting. These pews weren't fancy and did not have the swinging doors at the end. The cheap seats were all I could think of at the time. Apparently, there was a caste system alive and well in the Canadian Catholic Church in the early 1970s. The theory was that the more money you gave the church, the closer to the front and to God you got. I was so glad they didn't uphold these rules at St. Thomas in Peabody, or the Browns would have been sitting on the sidewalk every Sunday.

When we got back to the motel, my mother once again went up to the owner and said, "Again you fooled me. Why didn't you tell me that everyone owned their own pew?" This time, the proprietor just smiled and shyly said, "I didn't know." She explained that although prostitution might be legal in Canada, it was not highly looked upon by proper Catholics. Once she chose this lifestyle, she was excommunicated and not allowed to attend mass at St. Theresa. She didn't want pity or sympathy because she made her choice to stay home and raise her children. Giving up a brick building was a small price to pay to raise her children and put all four of them through college. Doris and the Madam had more in common than they knew.

While my father loaded the car for the next part of our adventure, my mother was saying goodbye. Doris gave our hostess a big hug and said it was an experience that she would never forget. My mother shared our hostess' belief that when you are a mother, your children's welfare always comes first, since it is a mother's duty to work, and care for her children no matter what personal sacrifices she must make. My mother continues to tell people about the night the Browns spent in a French Whore house.

Good Old USA

It took Doris awhile to get over the experiences of our last Canadian vacation. There was the blood poison in her leg in Montreal and the night in a French Whore House in Quebec. When she started her quest for a location for the next vacation she knew one thing: it was going to be in the good old U.S.A. A place where everyone spoke English was just a plus. The big question was, where? There were 48 continental states and so many places to visit and so much to see. Where would we go next?

I guess since we were getting older, Doris asked for our input this time around. She asked for our opinions and suggestions as to what we wanted to visit and explore. Also, we had already sold the trailer in Maine and this was really the only vacation we were going to have.

Junior was really into U.S. history and he wanted to see our nation's capital, Washington, D.C. There was the Smithsonian Museum, Lincoln's Memorial and the US Mint. But he couldn't stop there, Gettysburg, Pennsylvania, for all the Civil War history.

Toney was young, but he was already a sports fanatic. To him any city that housed a sports Hall of Fame would be perfect. So Cooperstown, N.Y. was chosen for the location of the Baseball Hall of Fame.

I, at the other end of the spectrum, really didn't care as long as we had a few days of relaxing at a pool or lake. We would be in New York State, so why not include Lake George for a few days of relaxing on the way home? Armed with all of this collective information, it was downloaded into the Doris mainframe computer. Since there was nothing close to a personal computer in the mid seventies that meant utilizing her brain, maps, camping guides and a lot of woman hours at the kitchen table. The next Brown, semi-annual vacation was hatched.

Doris now worked full time in a leather factory as a bookkeeper. She was the only one in the office, a one-girl operation as she called it. Her duties included bookkeeper, payroll, coffee maker, gofer, and toilet bowl cleaner. On a rare occasion, she was asked to baby-sit for the boss' children. She never minded because he was good to her. When her children needed jobs to help pay for their college education, he was more than happy to hire them in the factory as summer help. Tossing leather skins all day in 101-degree heat and the smell of rotten eggs never felt like a benefit to my brother and me.

Money wasn't as tight now, so our trips had moved up the ladder of luxury. We tented 50% of the time in campgrounds and 50% in inexpensive motels that all looked the same: just a long narrow building, one window and door every 20 feet to signify a room for rent. There was also that lonely parking space assigned to each door number. We also started to eat about 50% of our meals out at fast food, drive-thru or Howard Johnson-type restaurants. For a girl who could count on one hand how many times she had eaten in restaurants where there was actually a waitress, this was a monumental improvement.

We still had the maroon, 1968 Ford station wagon, and thank God we had a few more 8-track tapes to choose from for this trip. Newer technology and the cassette tape was replacing the 8 track. Doris picked up a dozen really cheap at the local department store where they were fazing them out.

This time we left from our house in Peabody and gave the neighbors quite a show. We had a special luggage carrier on the roof, and even though we camped less, we seemed to have more stuff. The back was packed to capacity floor to ceiling with the magic cooler easily accessible when you opened the back hatch. We were on our way, destination Washington D.C. and estimated time of arrival around 6 P.M. We were already booked into a motel for the first night in Alexandria, Virginia. Doris didn't want to take any chances we wouldn't have a place to stay, but little did she know it was directly under the flight path to what is now Regan International airport. There was a lesson to be learned, "Beware of the dangers of super cheap motel rooms," or as Doris learned, "Just travel with ear plugs."

We got there without any car or family mishaps; it was short of a miracle. I think it helped to have plenty of F.M. music stations along the way to keep Doris from firing up the 8 tracks. We were all checked into the motel and Doris decided to get the most of our time in D.C. We would take a paid tour the next day to see all the sites. Day three we would drive to the Smithsoian ourselves and spend the day. She was concerned about my father driving in the traffic and not knowing where he was going. My mother felt this was probably the safest way to see the city. Oh, she was going to find out how wrong she was.

The following morning, we went down to the dining room off of the lobby and had our wonderful continental breakfast. It was included in the price of the room and offered hot and cold cereals, pastries, fresh fruit and yogurt. What more could you want? So what if there had been a little plane noise during the night? The planes flew so low you could actually read the name of the airline on the side of the plane.

At 8:45 A.M., we gathered at the lobby. There were three families and a total of 15 adults and children all excited to take our tour. Within minutes, a stretch van that seated 16 showed up at the motel's front door. The name on the side said "Southern Tours." and the combination driver /tour guide got out. He was approximately 5 ft. 8 in. tall, medium build with grey hair and moustache. When he introduced himself as Geoffrey Southerbe, his accent was definitely southern, only I wasn't sure from which state. We didn't have to wait long because he said, "I hail from the great state of Georgia. Now, are all you folks Yankees?" I thought this was part of his routine, considering where we were and all the history. It was quickly apparent this wasn't any part of an act or tour.

Thank God the van was air conditioned because it had to be 98 degrees in the shade. Also, it probably saved all our lives because Geoffrey was rather verbal while he drove and at least the windows were closed to muffle his comments. The traffic getting into the city was some of the worst bumper-to-bumper I had ever seen. This was one of the reasons I knew my mother didn't want Dad to drive; his temper when he was in traffic was explosive. This guy made my father look like a pussycat.

Geoffrey was using profanities and flashing lude gestures, and I thought we were going to die. He started to call a black man in the car next to us the "n word" and pulled out a Billy club from under his seat. We were at a stop in traffic and Geoffrey put the transmission into park. He started to get up as though he was going to open our door that swung outward like a commuter bus when Doris stepped in. She was sitting in the first seat to his right, closest to the door.

Doris stood up and started yelling at Mr. Southerbe, "What the hell do you think you are doing? I am sick of the language you are using in front of the women and children in this van, and you call yourself a Southern gentleman? Sit down now! I did not come to Washington D.C. to have some crazy, tour guide get me killed because he can't control his mouth and his temper." Geoffrey was speechless. I don't think anyone ever told him about those full-blooded, Portuguese, Yankee women that hailed from Massassachusetts. He had made the supreme mistake of putting

Doris' children's lives in danger. It was like he came out of a trance. He apologized to everyone and put the club back under the seat.

The rest of the day was pretty uneventful. We saw the Lincoln, Jefferson and Washington memorials. Geoffrey turned out to be a very knowledgable tour guide when it came to anything about D.C. or the South. The tour Doris had chosen only had drive-bys of the White House and The Capital due to the time restraints. We went out to Arlington National Cemetery and saw both the tomb of the Unknown Soldier and President Kennedy's gravesite with the eternal flame. Finally, we ended our day with a tour of the U.S. Mint. It was really interesting to see how our money was manufactured. Unfortunately, they don't give out samples. All and all, the day turned out to be very informative and quiet after Doris took the bus driver on.

We spent day three at the Smithsonian Museum and I thought Junior would die. As we entered the enormous foyer, he said, "So much to see and so little time." I was amazed at how enormous it was. My favorite area was the exhibit hall that housed all the First Ladies' Inaugural ball gowns. I had a lot more fun than I thought I would. Doris had had mixed feelings about our tour the previous day when she realized that everything in Washington D.C. was free. We literally paid hard-earned money for a bigoted, red-necked, mentally deranged van driver. The next day it was off to Gettysburg and more history. Doris was going to wing it in Pennsylvania since our last tour guide was more than she had bargained for.

First thing to do in Pennsylvania was to set up the tent for the next two nights and pray for no rain. Doris, who usually waited until we got somewhere before we picked a place to stay, had already booked reservations at a nice campground a mile from the battleground. I think she never wanted to end up in a house of ill repute again. The next morning, bright and early, the battle began.

We followed the signs to where to park and headed to the large amphitheater in the round. There we would get our free map, and a short presentation on what was available to see. Once inside the two-story building, we were directed up two flights of stairs to a second-floor balcony. Everyone just took a position standing at the railing and looked below. There was a miniature scale model of the entire battlefield that was approximately 50 feet long and 25 feet wide. It was painted in greens and browns and had all the correct topography to signify hills, fields and trees. What happened next was a shock.

Without warning, the room went black and a male voice with a definite Southern drawl directed our attention below. The entire model came alive with a light show. I was oblivious as to what anything meant, but for the next 20 minutes we were with the Confederate and Union troops and were in the actual battle of Gettysburg. Junior was mesmerized and took in every word. When it finally came to an end, I was thrilled that we were done. What I hadn't realized was it was just the beginning.

When we had all exited the building, I thought, great, we saw the battle and now we can go back to the pool. I had missed somewhere in the show that it was merely the introduction and my brother was just getting started. Junior had just completed his study of the Civil War in his U.S. history class and he wanted to see everything. He pulled out his free paper map and we were off to walk and experience the battlefield. The time when I used to enjoy playing army with my brothers was long over. He was like an official tour guide, spurting facts and details that were not on the map. I always knew my brother was a genius with an I.Q. around 140. I just hadn't realized he also had a photographic memory. Those lights on the model that went on and off had actually meant something. It was the entire battle, who started where, who attacked who, and all the men who had died fighting for what they believed in.

It wasn't that I didn't care. I just hadn't had U.S. History in school yet and most of what he was saying was boring to a 13-year-old girl. I apparently wasn't the only one, since Toney was off with my father sitting under a tree. Doris could sense the boredom so she came up to me and said, "Hang in there. If we listen to Junior, I will treat you with dinner out tonight and dessert." Doris knew to get to my heart was always through my stomach. Well, I actually learned more than I thought, and it got better as people who joined our little tour group asked questions and Junior knew all the answers.

The tour of historic Gettysburg was finally over and it was time to choose a restaurant. This was a treat because almost 90% of our meals came out of Doris' magic cooler. The shapes and colors of the cooler changed over the years as they wore out from overuse. It often reminded me of the movie *Mary Poppins* when Mary keeps pulling things, even a floor lamp, out of her magic carpet bag. Instead of a lamp, Doris would create three course meals off the tailgate of the station wagon.

We started every trip with ice bricks that she made in our freezer using cleaned out, half-gallon milk containers. Doris felt that the ice lasted much longer than cubes and the melted water could be poured off from time to time preventing the food from getting wet. It was such a great idea that the owner of the campground started selling them along with the cubes for drinks. Once again an idea Doris created, but not one to profit from, how could you patent ice?

An example of a typical lunch would have been Italian sub (grinder) sandwiches with potato salad, and they would be created from scratch. Doris would pull out all the necessary ingredients: Deli cheese, ham, salami and mortadella, then slice a fresh tomato, onion and lettuce leaves. The five pounds of potato salad was prepared before we left home using a vinegar base and mayonnaise was only added to what we used, so there was no chance of salmonella. Out came the white paper plates that were the bargain variety, a little thicker than a paper napkin. Doris set up using the assembly line method. She would apply all the meat and cheese to the five rolls then you could add the veggies of your choice.

The finale would be a can of ice-cold soda to wash it all down. We only received soda (referred to as tonic in the state of Massachusetts) as a special treat on vacations. They were always the 12 for a $1 store variety, no brand names for us. Doris felt brands like Coke were too expensive and what kid is going to know the difference, cola was cola. At home it was always cheaper by the gallon Kool Aid.

The family had cleaned up, changed our clothing and we were on our way out for a special dinner. Doris had included many more meals out during our vacation, but dessert was still considered an extravagance. So we made a short detour to the local grocery chain and Doris purchased the surprise dessert to have later at the campground. It was placed in the cooler so it meant that it had to be kept cold. Did Doris buy my favorite, an ice cream cake? I did have to endure those hours of my brother and his intense Civil War lesson. The only way I was going to find out, was to get the dinner at the restaurant over with and hurry back to the campground.

Since I used to be a sugar addict and could never wait for a surprise, I was compelled to peak into the cooler. No one was shocked when I entered the back seat behind the driver carrying a box. My intention had been only to peak at it. When I went to the back of the car and gently removed the box that housed a Sara Lee six-layer chocolate cake with strawberry filling and whip cream frosting, I lost all self control. Doris knew me better than anyone, so looking out the windshield, never turning around to check, she said, "Don't open it up until we get back to the campground." How did she know?

The campground was only 10 minutes away, it was still 90 degrees at 9 P.M. and the car had no air conditioning. This was a recipe for disaster. I managed to loosen the lid and got one finger in for a tiny taste. I didn't want the taste as much as I wanted to tease my baby brother sitting next to me. It was the Ha, Ha, I have something you can't have mentality. What I was not aware of, while I was tormenting Toney, was that the beautiful cake was having some mechanical difficulties. Due to the temperature in the car, the six layers were starting to slide to one side and the frosting was pooling in the bottom of the box. I thought, oh No, they are going to kill me for ruining the dessert.

My brain was just forming the thought, "Maybe I should have Dad stop the car and put the cake back into the cooler," when all hell broke loose. On this dark two-lane highway, a large animal the size of a raccoon ran out into the road right in front of the car. Dad, who had always said, "The only good animal, is a dead animal," hit the brakes and we all went flying around the back seat. I can't remember if we actually had seat belts in the car, I only know we were not wearing them.

What happened wasn't my fault. What ever possessed him to suddenly stop the car and save the life of the defenseless animal? The sudden deceleration of the car had sent my melting Sara Lee six-layer chocolate cake with strawberries and whip cream frosting to become airborne. It left the box that I was still holding in my lap and landed, plastered to the back of Dad's head. Due to the adrenalin and shock of the animal in the road, there was a short, 10-second delay before Dad realized he was covered in cake. Then he started to yell profanities about the animal in the road and how he should have run it over. He blamed Doris for getting him into this situation, since she had purchased the cake.

We were all sitting very still and quiet in the back seat listening to our Dad carry on when suddenly from the front seat Doris started to laugh. She turned to look at my father with the brown cake like a wig on his head and started to laugh uncontrollably. My mother wasn't afraid of Dad's yelling when there was cake to be had. Doris had one of those laughs that made her whole face contort into these goofy expressions. You couldn't help but laugh at the faces she made and would end up laughing with her. What she did next shocked everyone. Doris leaned over and grabbed a big piece of cake that rested on the back of the seat and ate it. Well, I wasn't going to miss out so I scooped a handful with the whip cream and shoved it into my mouth. Oh it was just as good as I thought it would be. The feeding frenzy began and everyone grabbed for a piece before it melted totally. It wasn't long before the whole cake had been devoured.

My Dad didn't really see the humor of the situation until he was back at the campsite and all cleaned off. Dad swore from that day on, all desserts would be eaten outside of the car. They would consist of cookies, or could be frozen if individually wrapped and eaten immediately upon purchase. This was his assurance that he would never wear a chocolate confectionary hat again.

The rest of the trip was rather uneventful. We made our way to Cooperstown, N.Y. and the Baseball Hall Of Fame. Toney had the most fun among all the greats from baseball, especially the "Babe." We took a Polaroid picture of Toney in a pose holding a tiny bat standing next to the plaque honoring Babe Ruth. Of everywhere we had been on our vacations, Cooperstown is the location Toney recently took his family back to. There he repeated the same pose holding a slightly larger bat, next to The Babe's plaque. The two pictures sit side by side on Doris' refrigerator door that has become her family photo gallery. The 8-year-old boy and the 42-year-old man: some things really never ever change. Or do they?

The first time Toney was at Cooperstown, The Boston Red Sox had not won a Worlds Series championship since 1918, when Babe Ruth put the curse on the team for selling him to the

Yankees. What fan could blame him? He returned the year the curse was broken and the Boston Red Sox were the 2004 World Series Champions. When it comes to sports obsessions, I would say that Toney is most like his father. The only difference is that he uses sports to spend time with his son and family, not to get away from them.

Doris even did a 360 degree turn around toward sports after she divorced my father. I think she had resented the professional sports teams because of my father's obsession. He ignored his wife and children to sit in front of the TV for hours at a time. He would be golfing all day Sunday and had left many family events over the years, such as my First Communion, in order to be in a golf tournament. What Doris finally learned was that the problem wasn't the sporting events; the problem was her husband. Once she removed the problem in 1975, my mother once again started to enjoy sports and life.

Today in her 80's, she would never miss a Red Sox game on TV or the opportunity to join her son at a live game at Fenway Park. The New England Patriots hold a special place in her heart since they were the first stock she had ever purchased. The fact that they have won three Super Bowl Championships in the last few years has nothing to do with it. Doris will tell you that although she loves Tom Brady, she is not going to freeze her ass off to sit in Gillette Stadium to see a game in person. A warm living room, a comfortable chair and a Sam Adams in her hand, and she is a happy camper.

Doris Takes In Strays

Doris had eight jobs total in her entire lifetime. She started at the Sylvania Lighting Plant making light bulbs during World War II and continued for a few months after high school graduation. That is when she decided to go to business school, for a 2-year bookkeeper certificate. Math had always been her best subject throughout high school and the only A's she ever received. Doris didn't like the rigidity of working on an assembly line in a factory for the rest of her life. Punch in, punch out, when the whistle sounded 15-minute break or 30-minute lunch. She could only go to the bathroom when a whistle blew, and she refused to be treated like a trained animal.

Following graduation from business school, she landed a job at an exclusive woman's clothing store in Salem, Massachusetts. At a time when a dress could be purchased for $5, the dresses in this shop were hundreds. Doris was one of the bookkeepers in the office doing accounts receivable. Her boss was a very wealthy man from Beacon Hill, Boston and friendly with the high society of the country.

Doris was never sure why her boss liked her. I think it was her genuine honesty. He probably dealt with phony people every day that had hidden agendas, and Doris was a breath of fresh air. What you saw is what you got. She wasn't prim and proper, but put her in a $200, black, silk jersey dress and she could compete with the best of them, at least on the outside.

There was a particular customer that was a little larger than she wanted to be and would always try to get clothes in a smaller size than she took. The sales women worked on commission and would lie to her and say she looked great when Doris knew she didn't. When this certain rich lady called to say she would be in, Doris told her to come at a time when she knew the sales lady was at lunch. She changed the tags from size 14 to size 10 on many items that she felt would look good on her. The woman arrived, and Doris had all the clothes she had chosen in the dressing room for her to try on. The larger sizes fit her so well, and she looked great. The customer was so happy with how she looked that she bought six outfits. The boss found out what Doris had done because the sales woman came in just as the customer was leaving weighted down with packages. Doris told him how she watched the sales help sell her clothing that looked terrible on her just to get a commission. He wasn't as mad with Doris as he was with his staff for lying to his customers.

Doris worked for this man for almost five years and left the day she got the call from the adoption agency that she could pick up her son that following week. He was so happy for Doris that she was finally going to become a mother that he helped get all the baby furniture to her house and set up the nursery. Another boss might have been angry with an employee for just walking out; I think he loved my mother like a daughter.

Doris had a few part-time jobs through the years to pay for specific vacations or home projects, and they only lasted a few months at a time. One summer, she worked in a glue factory on the assembly line again, packing boxes with cans of glue. One Christmas she took a night job at a department store to get money for gifts, and it was only for six weeks. It wasn't until 1968 and the start of private high school tuition bills that she returned to a 40-hour-a-week job as a bookkeeper in a leather factory.

This owner was not as understanding with Doris. His sister worked in the office, and she made my mother's life a living hell. One day Doris came home from work early, and I knew something was wrong. She took my hand and said, "I have to tell someone: I just quit my job. I can't stand that bitch for one more day." Sometimes she did things spontaneously without any thought and sometimes it worked out for the best. It got back to Doris that after she left, the boss' sister couldn't keep up with the workload. Doris had been doing both jobs, and the boss now understood who the real problem had been. My mother wouldn't go back even when he called and offered her more money. One thing that Doris had was self respect and no money was worth giving it up.

It was all for the best because the very next week there was an advertisement in the local newspaper for a bookkeeper. It was a job that sounded custom-made for my mother. The ad read: "Bookkeeper needed, one-woman office in a small leather factory, experience in accounts receivable and payable, as well as payroll." The address listed was just down the street from our house. Maybe things in life do happen for a reason.

Doris was so excited; she showered, got dressed and drove to the building without even calling first. At this time, you went to the job site listed and physically filled out an application. There was no internet, e-mail or faxes; it was the old fashioned paper and pencil method. She parked in the lot next door and entered the door with a sign that said "office entrance" with an arrow pointing up. The stairs were narrow in width, and the wooden treads had a worn pattern up the centers that made them feel unsteady. They ended in a small corridor, and directly in front was a sliding window with an office sign written above it. There she caught site of a buzzer and pressed it for a few seconds.

Out came a very handsome young man in his late 20's, with hazel eyes and shoulder length auburn hair, and asked, "Can I help you?" Doris had just started to explain when a slightly overweight young woman in a long gauzy, yellow peasant dress followed him into the office and said, "Hi, I'm Lisa, his wife. Are you here for the bookkeeper job?" Doris replied, "Yes." Immediately the young woman led her into the office. I think she almost got hired on the spot.

What Doris was not privy to was that her new boss wanted to hire his own bookkeeper. His wife Lisa had arrived 30 minutes prior and found him interviewing a 21-year-old blonde in a mini skirt. So when Doris, age 48, salt and pepper hair, wearing long pants and loose-fitting jersey came to the window, she fit the profile that his wife was looking for. She was interviewed and hired 45minutes later. Her new boss seemed a little disappointed, but he found out later that she was an excellent bookkeeper. She was familiar with the leather business, payroll, spoke three languages, and she had great people skills. The one and only qualification his wife was interested in was that she wasn't looking to have an affair with her rich 28-year-old husband.

Matt The Rat

Doris worked at that leather factory for over 16 years until she retired in 1984. The entire time she was there she took care of everyone. Her young boss became like one of her children, and she made sure he stopped to have lunch and usually walked downtown to get it. He in turn gave her children, Junior and me, jobs during the summer to help us defray our college costs. She was so grateful because she was now a single mother and had two kids in college this particular year. I didn't think we were all that lucky when our friends were going to the beach and we were in a 100-degree factory from 7 A.M.–3:30 P.M. I guess I was grateful at the end of the summer because I had made $6 per hour when minimum wage was $1.85 per hour, which ensured I could pay all my school expenses and not have to work during the school year.

The factory life is not an easy one, especially if you had been doing it for your whole life and the only way out was retirement or death. I felt it was the closest thing I could experience to being in jail with a life sentence, only for me there was the possibility of parole in September. The factory was a leather-finishing facility so there were actually three jobs available on the assembly line for a non-machinist. The choices were, throw the raw 4×4 foot suede skins onto the conveyor belt, apply and spread the thick chemical finish with a large paddle, or hang and remove the dry skins from the dryer. To say it was boring and monotonous is an understatement. This job was my life eight hours a day, five days a week for 12 long weeks.

The conditions were inhumane at times, with temperatures reaching up to 110 degrees, and the only air conditioning was in Doris' office. The boss had plenty of cold-water jugs that were filled each day and all the salt tablets you wanted to swallow to keep from dehydrating. Sometimes the organic solvents used to coat the leather skins would smell like sulfur or rotten fish, and they were overpowering. My mother considered our ability to work in the factory as a fringe benefit of her job. The only benefit I could see was when it was over and I went back to school in September.

Some of the characters that I worked with had criminal records. Others had minimal formal education, and the rest were hard-working immigrants. There was Lester the molester. He was tall and gaunt, had long greasy blonde hair and was missing a few top teeth. Thank God he was arrested and never came back two weeks after I started. I never asked what the charges were because I was afraid to know.

We had Manual Labor, who was in his late 50's and had worked his entire life in this country in factories. He would arrive every morning carrying his lunch pail, dressed in a clean, pressed shirt and slacks, and would change into work clothes for the day. At the end he would shower, change back into his clean clothes and walk home. He was dependable and never missed a day of work in the previous 10 years.

Then there was Matt, affectionately referred to as Matt the Rat. He wasn't that tall, about 5 ft. 8 in., and what he lacked in height he made up for in bulging muscles. He was most proud of his biceps and the tattoo on the right one. It was a four-inch long, cartoon-like rat figure with large fangs and blood dripping from its mouth. To show it off he always wore shirts with the sleeves torn off. Matt was dark skinned and had straight, shoulder-length, jet-black hair that was always tied back with a bandana. He attributed his appearance to his mother's Cherokee Indian heritage.

Everyone in the factory was afraid of Matt. If he asked or told someone to do something, they did it without any arguments. Doris, on the other hand, felt pity, not fear. Doris believed that he didn't get enough love and attention being one of 12 children, so she spoiled him. Her theory was that everyone needed love and attention, even a tough guy like Matt.

Twice a week Doris would take a sandwich order from the guys and gals in the shop and call it in around 11 A.M. Then she would leave for her daily walk downtown to do the errands and pick up the order on her way back. This allowed the workers to sit outside in the shade and enjoy the entire 30-minute lunch break without wasting time at the sandwich shop. Doris saw to it that Matt always got extra. Sometimes it would be sliced tomatoes from her garden or something she had baked the night before. When she handed it to him, she would say, "You look thin, you're not eating enough." Everyone knew that Matt did drugs, including Doris, and this was her way to let him know that she cared.

One day it had to be 110-degrees in the building and everyone was getting five minute breaks every hour for extra water and salt pills. I was feeding the conveyor belt and Matt was the first one in line applying the soup. I had been drinking a lot of water, but I didn't take any salt pills. I had developed this phobia about pills and choking so I couldn't swallow them. It proved to be a big mistake. The last thing I remembered, the people on the assembly line were getting wavy and I went to turn and grab another leather skin and the world went black. This was the first time in my life that I had ever swooned.

People told me after I woke up what had happened. All I remember is opening my eyes and there was Matt. He apparently had seen me starting to go and had jumped over the platform and caught me before I hit the machinery or the floor. He lifted me onto the soft bale of suede skins and was yelling, "Get Doris, someone get F—ing Doris." I opened my eyes and Matt had my hand in his and he was patting it. He asked me if I was all right. He had already poured some cold water on a bandana from his pocket and put it on my forehead. I remember looking up at him and laughing. There was Mr. Hell's Angel patting my hand and freaking out. Doris arrived and I was starting to come back. Doris and Matt helped me into her air-conditioned office and she wet my clothes to cool me down. I got a lecture on taking in salt tablets and then she drove me home.

I could see what my mother saw when she looked into Matt's eyes and his kind soul. I recovered and learned to swallow pills, so we didn't have any more excitement on the line. Matt had his own excitement at home later that week. The 17-year-old girl he was living with had his baby girl the night before. Matt had called in because he was still at the hospital, and told the boss he would be into work the next day.

When Doris got to the office the following day at 8 A.M. she ran into the factory to see if Matt had come to work. There he was at the first position on the assembly line, next to me. So she congratulated him on the birth of his daughter and asked, "Where are the pictures?" He promised to come to her office at the 9 A.M. break, and show her.

His girlfriend had to have a Cesarean Section because the labor did not progress easily. The baby was born Wednesday at 10:00 P.M., healthy and weighed in at 6 lbs. 9 oz., 19 inches long. He showed us the first delivery picture that the hospital takes. She actually resembled Matt with long black hair and pudgy cheeks. Doris confirmed that she was the most beautiful baby she had ever seen.

That night, after work, Doris and I went to the local department store and bought the baby a few things. We got T shirts, two stretch terry pajamas, receiving blankets, tiny socks, a sweater and a white eyelet bonnet. Everything a newborn baby girl needed to come home from the hospital. We assumed that the hospital would supply a few diapers and bottles of formula, as well as the essentials, like powder, soap and shampoo. We actually wrapped all the gifts in the car right in the parking lot and drove directly to the maternity unit.

It was still visiting hours so we felt calm about going. When we went up to the desk and asked for the room number, we got a strange look from the nurse. When we got to the room, Matt was there, but the baby was back in the nursery to be fed. Since the mother had surgery she was feeling sore and tired, so she had just asked the nurse to take the baby so she could get some sleep.

Matt was stubborn about the fact that he wanted Doris to hold the baby. So Doris devised a compromise. We would look at the baby through the glass tonight and visit them at their apartment the next weekend. He finally agreed since it was getting late and we had to be back at work at 7 A.M. the next morning.

Two weeks later, we made arrangements with Matt on Friday afternoon to be at his apartment at 1 P.M. the next day. He wrote the address down and I was confident I could find it. The neighborhood at that time could be classified as an urban slum. The streets were very narrow with alternating one way streets going both east/west and north/south. There was an equal mix of enormous multi-unit brick apartment houses that took over city blocks and smaller three to six family wooden tenement houses. There was very little on street parking available.

Doris and I were in my yellow, 1972, Plymouth Scamp with its brown vinyl roof. I wasn't sure which end of the large street he lived at, so it took us a couple passes around the block to locate the apartment house. It was a massive, six story tall, red brick building, with windows on all sides. The style was vintage post-World War II construction and there were many of them in the neighborhood. Locating the building was only the first problem.

I decided to park right in front. At least there weren't any No Parking signs visible, so hopefully we wouldn't get ticketed or towed. I suddenly became aware of two groups of young men at opposite corners from the building. To the right were five black males, ages 16 to early 20s, and they were just standing there, looking at us. Six young Hispanic males were on the other corner, and they were also just staring at our car. Now I was starting to get a little worried. Forget about a ticket, would there be a car left when we came out from Matt's?

I leaned over to my mother and said, "Do we really want to do this?" She replied, "Get out of the car and don't forget to lock it." I just looked at Doris and laughed. Did she really think locking the doors was going to stop these thugs from stealing or vandalizing the car if they wanted to? We both got out, when I noticed the gangs starting to walk toward us. I was tempted to throw Doris back into the front seat and run, when I heard a wolf whistle. Could it be some war cry? Then I heard Matt's voice yell from above, "Doris, come on up, apartment 401." There he was hanging out over the windowsill from a fourth floor window. His chest was bare and he had on his signature black bandana over his hair. Doris turned to me and said, "What are you waiting for?"

I was in shock until I looked toward the two gangs and they were moving quickly in the opposite direction. I guess Matt the Rat had a reputation in the neighborhood. I was no longer worried about anyone touching my car or attacking us that day. Doris started walking toward the building like she was walking in the mall, perfectly calm.

We walked into the hall that was at least 10 feet wide, ran the entire length of the building and was dimly lit. To our right at the halfway point was a large wooden staircase leading both up and down. The solid oak banisters were carved, the treads were covered in grey linoleum and clean of debris. We started our climb to the fourth floor walk up.

Once we reached our destination I was a little winded and flushed. Doris looked like she could keep on going to the sixth floor. My mother was already walking 1–2 miles a day with her errands downtown and daily runs to the post office for the factory. We had reached the landing and there was Matt standing in an open doorway just waiting for us to arrive. Doris was off like a racehorse out of the gate; she couldn't wait to hold this bundle of joy. I was in the rear holding the bags of still more gifts.

I followed her into the apartment and closed the door. I was tempted to lock it behind me, but thought it might look suspicious. The apartment was immaculate and full of natural light since there were so many windows and no window treatments. Doris sat in a wooden kitchen chair at a small, round maple table in the center of the room we had just entered. There on the table was a car seat and the inhabitant was the most beautiful newborn baby girl I had ever seen. Her skin was flawless. She had rosy cheeks, a perfect spherical head covered in downy black hair, and wide charcoal eyes staring up at us. Matt scooped her up, using proper head technique and placed her gently in Doris' arms. It was love at first sight for both of them.

Doris started with her pet baby phrases, "cara linda," meaning "beautiful face" in Portuguese and her pet name for babies "Bedelia Co hogs." The baby could not take her black-as-night eyes off my mother. To this day, it amazes me how babies respond to Doris. She has always claimed it's her unique voice, but I think its because once you are wrapped in her arms she just generates so much love. We spent the better part of the afternoon visiting and left before dark. We never saw the baby again.

A few weeks later, Matt didn't show up for work on Monday and the guys were all talking in the break room. He hadn't called in and that was not like him. Doris knew something was not right. My mother went out into the factory and asked one of the guys he hung with where he was? He answered, "Doris, I'm sorry. Matt died in jail over the weekend of a drug overdose." He had been arrested and they just threw him into the holding tank. They found him later that morning, dead on the cot.

I could see the pain on my mother's face. Her eyes started to well up and she went back into her office and cried. Matt had been somebody's child, and they didn't give him enough love or attention to keep him safe. Then Doris started thinking and worrying about his baby. Matt's girlfriend was only 17 years old and rumor had it that she was also into drugs. What was going to happen to that beautiful baby girl? There wasn't really anything she could do. I wasn't going back to that apartment if Matt wasn't there to protect us.

Doris would frequently think of Matt and his tragic life. Later that year Doris found out, from one of the workers, that his girlfriend had sold the baby girl on the black market. Apparently there was a lot more to Matt the Rat than Doris even knew. He had been under surveillance by the authorities for drug trafficking. The strange looks we received when we had gone to the hospital to see the baby were due to the fact that all visitors were being investigated for drug connections. That fact made Doris smile, my mother the drug dealer.

There were children throughout Doris' life that she tried to help. In the early 1960's, my father's niece Mary came to live with us for five months. She was only 17 years old, had alabaster skin with a gentle covering of freckles and flaming red hair. Her mother had to leave her and her brother due to illness. According to Doris, the illness was that she was pregnant. Doris was very hard on parents who didn't do their job. She called my aunt a whore who thought more about sex than she did about the care of her children. She went away for five months while she had the child. At that time in history, it was still illegal to get an abortion and Roe vs. Wade had not passed yet. God knows whatever happened to that child. Doris prayed her sister-in-law put it up for adoption to give it a chance for happiness.

We managed to all fit into this tiny apartment with two bedrooms and now four children. My poor cousin had to sleep on the couch in the living room, and my mother drove her to high school every morning. I remember one evening Mary had not come home from school and Doris was frantic with worry. She was not used to this teenager stage, since my older brother was only 10 years old at the time. My cousin called on the phone to ask Aunt Doris if she could go to Manchester. Doris, not being good at geography, only thought of Manchester, N.H., over an hour away and started yelling into the phone: "No! You are not going anywhere. Do you know what time it is? You get your little ass back into this house right now!"

We were all afraid. What was Doris going to say and what was our cousin going to do when she got home? Mary was in front of our house in 10 minutes. Doris was standing at the front door, and when Mary walked in, she grabbed my mother in a giant hug and said, "This is the first time anyone ever cared if I was dead or alive." The fact that she had only wanted to go to Manchester, Massachusetts, only 10 minutes away, didn't matter anymore.

While she lived with us, she confided in Doris. Her mother had brought men home and tried to get Mary to have sex with them. They didn't have food in the house and her mother was sometimes gone for days. She had been taking care of her eight-year brother since her father left three years before. When it was time for Mary to return home, she begged my mother to keep her. Doris didn't have the room or finances to care for any more children.

Mary graduated from high school and lived nearby for a few years, and then we never heard from her again. Her younger brother went to live with his father and his new family. I see Mary's brother occasionally since he lives nearby. Once in a while, my mother will ask him if he has heard from Mary and the answer is always no. I can see the guilt that Doris carries and the unanswered questions she has. Where is she now? Is she still alive? Has she been happy? Does she have a family of her own? Doris will probably never have these questions answered.

The Rich Kid

I'm sure you have heard of the term "Babe Magnet"; Doris was a "Kid Magnet." I could never figure out why children just wanted to hang out at our 900-square-foot apartment, but they did. It wasn't decorated in high-end furniture, and Doris would joke and say her decorating style was early Morgan Memorial. Yes, we had a beautiful backyard with multiple fruit trees, roses, and peonies all around the perimeter. My grandfather was illiterate, but in the garden he was a genius. He had grafted multiple varieties of pears and apples on our trees. The pear tree had Bartlet, Bosc and Anjou varieties, and you just had to walk out into the yard and pick one. As a kid, in the summer, you would never go hungry.

When we stopped camping at Beach Acres in Maine, Doris knew that we needed something to keep us busy on summer vacation. She took the tax refund money that year and invested in an 18-foot, above ground swimming pool. It wasn't large, and laps were out of the question since it was round. My mother's only criteria was that she could stand up in it and not have the water be over her head, so it was only four feet deep. Doris couldn't swim and had no desire to learn. She would say that the purpose of the pool was after a hot day at work she could come home and cool her ass off in it.

The first summer we had the pool we had an unbearable July day that hit 95 degrees, with 100% humidity. Doris had come home from work and made a proclamation, "I am going into the pool." She donned her only bathing suit, a black floral with an attached skirt that had seen better days.

We were all in disbelief. But she walked out the breeze way that lead to the back yard, and kicked off her dollar flip flops. She started the climb up the aluminum ladder that led over the wall and into the pool.

Doris had started her descent and the reality of the situation hit us, she was going to actually wet her ass. Only with my mother things never go according to plan. No one knows what happened exactly, but suddenly there was a splash and she was gone. The 6 teenagers that were witness to the event ran to the side of the pool. What they saw left them speechless. Doris was sitting on the bottom of the four foot pool, distorted under the clear blue water with a steady steam of air bubbles coming to the surface. The guys all jumped in and lifted her up into a standing position and then passed her over the side onto solid ground.

Then came the all perplexing question. Mom, you are five foot 2 inches tall, the water is less than four feet deep, why didn't you just stand up? Her reply was, "I didn't know I could." She was in her forties and she had never been in a swimming pool. Doris would go to the beach, walk into the water ankle deep and right back out. She had never taken a swimming lesson and had no clue how to push at the water with her hands or hold her breath. When she realized what had happened and that she could have drowned if she had been alone, she never set foot into the pool again. To cool off meant sitting in the shade of the apple tree sipping a cold beverage, preferably one that contained alcohol.

The pool continued to draw in teenagers during the summer months. Or could it have been the fact that you could almost guarantee that a meal would be waiting when you arrived? Doris had the motto, "There was always enough for one more, just add another potato to the pot." She was always there to sit and listen to any problem a kid might have. Doris never judged, she only tried to be compassionate and offer what ever help she could. My mother had been a wild child and teenager, so she knew first hand "shit happens."

This summer, my brother's friend introduced a fellow college classmate to the Browns. He and his sister Stephanie were staying with their elderly grandmother for the summer just a few streets away. They were from California, and their dad was some rich movie producer and their mom was a small town girl who had made it to the big time. They had a Beverly Hills mansion, sent their only daughter to boarding school in England and their son, Darren, was attending college in Massachusetts.

Doris was entering a new phase in parenting called the teenage stage. My brother was 19 and I was 16 years old, and up until this summer, we really hadn't given Doris any problems with bad behavior or drug use. My mother wasn't naïve about what was available to her children to get them into trouble. She had also said on too many occasions to count, "You get arrested, have a nice vacation in jail because I don't have the money to bail you out."

Doris started smoking cigarettes when she was 17 years old in 1941. She was a senior in high school and there was a war on. Women were working in factories and taking on more male roles while the young men were at war. So if a man could smoke, why not Doris?

Her mother was a very domineering woman and was always implying her only daughter wasn't a "good" girl. Teodolinda suspected that Doris was smoking, so she would smell her clothing when she came home from an evening out with friends. Doris' excuse was that her friends were smoking; it wasn't her. Her mother would search Doris' room because the house was hers and she could do anything she wanted in it. Only Doris was a very sly juvenile delinquent. She would hide her cigarettes in her mother's gray umbrella in her own bedroom closet. Doris never got caught because she always remembered to move the stash if it was going to rain and there was a hint that Teodolinda would use the umbrella.

I ask you, how were my siblings and I supposed to get away with anything when Doris had done it all when she was a kid? She had told us all the stories, so we knew if we hid anything she would find it. Doris wasn't as controlling as her mother. She did share the belief that the house was hers and she could search anything she wanted in it, regardless of whose it was. Then there was facing the "Wrath of Doris" if we got caught doing something illegal. You always had to weigh the benefit/punishment ratio to determine if it was really worth doing. Doris believed that a child should grow up with a healthy fear of their parents, and she had succeeded where I was concerned.

When Darren showed up, I started to wonder if a little trouble was worth the consequences to have some fun. It was love at first site. He was a California surfer boy with dirty blonde hair in tight ringlets down to his shoulders. His eyes were a topaz blue and he lacked a summer tan so you could still see the light brown freckles that dotted his complexion. He had trouble written all over his face.

My love life during my teenage years was non-existent. I used to blame it on the fact that I was a little chubby and was shy around boys. Looking back now, I wonder if it could have been something else. My brother's friends would call me a "Good Girl." I was the type a guy marries and doesn't date, which always confused me because how could I get married if no one would date me? Could it have been Doris' threats that anyone who tried to have sex with her only daughter would be castrated? Unfortunately, most people tended to believe what Doris said. I think that might have definitely been a hindrance to my popularity with boys.

There was another boy named Dougie that had been a classmate of mine since first grade, attended my high school and was working with my brother Junior at the mall. Dougie was over 6 feet tall, had long straight hair that hung into his eyes. He had rounded shoulders and a distinctive posture so when he walked it gave the impression he was looking down at the ground. I'm not sure how he got to my house, but one day he was at the front door with my brother after work and he never seemed to leave that summer. Dougie came from a broken home, as it was called in the 1970's. His parents had divorced when he was in seventh grade and he lived with his single mother.

He would tell us stories of coming home stoned after smoking pot, his eyes bloodshot, and his mother would ask if his allergies were bothering him. She always seemed to be self-absorbed and I wondered if she had her own substance abuse problem. Sometimes he would spend the night and I never saw him call her and she never called looking for him. Doris would have the police out if we were 15 minutes late and she hadn't received a call. Dougie's mother didn't seem to care where her son was or what he was doing.

On this July evening, Darren and Dougie, who had met at our house, showed up together at supper time. It was 93 degrees and no one had air conditioning in the good old days, so the pool might have been the reason for their appearance. While he was eating, Darren developed killer hiccups. His sudden uncontrollable muscle twitches and gasps almost caused Darren to choke on his food. There were at least six people over that night and everyone had his or her own hiccup remedy.

He started with: Just take a deep breath, hold your nose and stop breathing until you think you'r going to pass out. He made a few attempts at this method, but the results were always the same, hiccup. The next suggestion was to breathe into a paper bag for five minutes. I had been under the assumption the paper bag had been the treatment for hyperventilation, not hiccups. Things were not working, and poor Darren was laughing so hard and hiccupping that he was clutching his abdomen.

Doris came to the rescue with her foolproof cure for hiccups. Take a large glass, fill it to the half mark with water, hold the glass in front of you and tip it away from your body, bend over placing you mouth on the rim that is away from you and tip the glass up until you can gulp or slurp the water into your mouth, and swallow. The directions were very confusing, so Doris gave a visual demonstration. Now Darren was ready, glass of water in hand and an audience watching him.

I think what happened next was the "Scare the hell out of you method" because when Darren bent over, something fell out of his shirt pocket. He was so busy slurping that he didn't see what had happened or the fact that the room had become very quiet. When Darren stood up, he looked a little confused. Why weren't people laughing? Then he saw what had fallen out of his breast pocket: two joints and a small bag of marijuana, just sitting on the kitchen floor. He was about to see an example of "The Wrath Of Doris" first hand.

No one said a word. Doris bent down and carefully picked up the stuff off the floor. With a stern face and controlled slow speech she said, "There will be no drugs, reefers in my house. You are still welcome here, but don't you dare ever bring any kind of drugs into my house again. Do I make myself clear?" With that Darren apologized to Doris and made her a promise that he wouldn't do it again. She gave him back his drugs and a long lecture on the dangers of smoking marijuana. I once again received the added lecture that if you get arrested for drug possession, you can never be a nurse. That was all I needed to hear. I wanted to be a nurse more than I wanted Darren to like me. I think this was Doris' way of helping me put my life priorities in order.

The summer was one of the best I ever had. I was able to hangout with Darren and popular kids and see how the other half lived. Everyone continued to come to the house all summer, and they kept their promise to Doris: no drugs, reefers (as she called them) or being stoned at her house. That isn't to say they didn't do drugs, just not in Doris' presence. I did hang out with them occasionally when they were smoking weed, and I got very good at rolling a joint. To this day, I can honestly say I have never tried any illegal drugs. Being a nurse was more important to me than any summer romance could ever be. Plus I always had to sit downwind when they smoked because the smell of cannabis made me physically sick.

Many years later, when Doris was still working at the leather factory and walked downtown to perform some errands, she thought she saw Dougie. She was almost in tears when she called me on the phone because of what she saw. This man was in his late 20s, long dirty hair pulled back into a pony tale, torn jeans and flip-flop sandals. She was on the opposite side of the street and was afraid to go over to him in case she was wrong and this was some crazy street person. As she watched him walk away, there were those rounded shoulders and his signature walk, still looking down at the sidewalk.

The Homeless Laborer

When Doris was hired as a bookkeeper at the leather factory, she also took on other titles. She was the office interpreter for the many Portuguese and Hispanic workers over the years. She was a glorified gofer, running downtown everyday to get the mail, pick up lunch orders and dry cleaning. At times she was the office medical provider, taking care of minor problems such as administering aspirin for a hangover or dressing minor wounds. A role that Doris imposed upon herself was that of surrogate mother to anyone who needed to be mothered.

On a sunny Monday morning in June, Doris was sitting at her old wooden desk amid piles of paper and payroll sheets when a young, dark, handsome man appeared at her interoffice window. Doris asked, "What can I do for you?" He replied, "I am here to start work." Before Doris could reach the door to let him in, her boss was there in her office welcoming him. The office portion of the factory was comprised of two 12×18 foot adjoining rooms with a door between that was rarely closed. Her boss seemed to be expecting him and called him by name, Juan. The new laborer was led through the door into the inner private office and the door closed instantly.

Doris had a feeling there was something strange about this laborer. He was clean-shaven, and smelled of Irish Spring soap as he passed her, yet he wore old jeans and a worn T-shirt with the word Budweiser on the front. It wasn't unusual for the boss to hire young college students that were the children of his wealthy friends to give them a taste of the real world. It was always a successful lesson and resulted in the student happily returning to college in the fall. This man, however, seemed a little older than the others.

Every morning at 7 A.M., Juan arrived to work. Monday through Friday, and every afternoon he walked downtown and disappeared. He didn't have a car and there were no hotels nearby, just a few rooming houses and apartment buildings. The mystery was killing Doris and she had to know. She tried to find an application in the file and there wasn't one. When it came to do the biweekly pay, his name and payroll number were handwritten onto the list and a W-2 form was left on her desk. Doris had no way to find out who he was and where he came from.

Doris believed being direct was always the best method, to get information. So the next day when she saw him, she asked, "Juan, where do you live?" He quickly answered, "The rooming house two blocks away. That's why I walk every day. I don't need a car." That immediately blew the "kid of a rich friend" theory out of the water, since he was living in a rooming house. Doris knew for sure that he was a foreigner from the accent, and Hispanic because she had heard him speak Spanish. It was confusing her because he was fluent in English and his grammar was impeccable. Juan was more grammatically correct when he spoke than she was. He must have been well educated, wherever he had come from.

Once she confirmed that he was living alone, she immediately assumed he must be lonely. Doris, having been an only child, felt that no one should ever be alone. He didn't seem to befriend anyone, and the guys in the factory didn't seem to be his type, so Juan became Doris' summer project that year. Doris started supplementing his lunch with fresh tomatoes from her garden and fruit from our trees. Since he lived in a rooming house, chances were he didn't have cooking facilities and that his meals were all takeout. Doris' motto was, "Fresh and homemade was always better than store bought." She fed a lot of the workers, especially if she felt they were too thin or doing too many drugs or booze. Doris' solution for any problem, from a simple headache to world peace, was to feed it away. Once Doris was happy that he was eating well, she decided to help him with his social life.

Doris estimated his age to be approximately 22–26 years old, and since she had a 19-year-old daughter and 22-year-old son at home, why not invite him to dinner? One Tuesday afternoon, as Juan was leaving for the night, she asked him to join us for dinner on Thursday at 5 P.M. and he accepted. If my father had still been living with us, he would have gone ballistic. Over the years Doris had invited a few interesting characters to our house for a meal and my father's reaction would always be the same. He would say, "Are you crazy? Do you really know these people? They could come back and rob us or be killers." Doris answered, "I know them well enough, and why would they come back to rob us when we don't have anything worth stealing?" So, once again, Doris threw caution to the wind and planned her menu.

Doris arrived home at 4:05 P.M. and completed the meal preparations. She had made stuffed peppers and tomatoes, from her own garden that morning, and just had to bake them. Like a lot of ethnic families in the area, we had a small kitchen in the basement. It was just a four-burner gas stove and oven with a small counter all nestled in next to the set tub and washer. It allowed Doris to cook all year round, even when hot weather would normally prohibit it. I helped her create a large garden salad using the Boston lettuce, cucumber and tomatoes, once again from our own garden. Dessert was one of Doris' specialty cream puffs, only in the summer she filled them with vanilla ice cream, chocolate sauce on top and a dab of fresh whipped cream. That morning, while she was preparing the main course, she baked the shells. Doris was the original prototype of the phrase "multi-tasking."

She had offered to pick Juan up at his room and he declined, saying he preferred to walk and he would have no problem finding our home. At 4:50 P.M. came a knock at the front door, right on time. Juan was in a clean, pressed, light blue chambray sports shirt, dark slacks and shiny black leather shoes. He didn't look the part of day laborer, nor did he look like the typical American male of 1977. At that time, bellbottom jeans, polyester leisure suits and platform shoes would have been the norm. He was also carrying a bottle of chilled white wine in a discrete brown paper bag.

We ate Doris' great three-course meal in our little kitchen with paper napkins and no formality, just served family style. She did put out her crystal wine glasses that she received as a wedding gift and they added a little bit of elegance to the table. What I learned later in life was if Doris was cooking, the only thing anybody cared about or needed was the food. It could be served on paper plates with plastic cutlery as long as Doris had created it.

It was such a beautiful summer evening, around 78 degrees, light westerly breeze and no humidity, so we decided to go sit in the backyard. As you walked through the breezeway door, you entered a fantasy garden. The lawn was dark green and plush. It was my younger brother's job to make sure of it. He continued to use the yellow push mower my grandfather had used for 40 plus years. Thank God the terrain was flat.

To the right was a sprawling apple tree that Joe, Doris' father, had planted the day they moved into the house in celebration of his first home and newborn daughter. He was a genius at grafting different plants and this tree had both Cortland's and Macintosh apples growing from different branches. By this time of the summer, the branches were drooping toward the ground laden with juicy apples. If Joe had lived in another generation, been educated, and with his natural talent, he could have been a horticulturalist. Instead, he was an immigrant who never learned to read or write and didn't make a lot of money, but he guaranteed his family would never go hungry.

The yard was like having a fresh produce market in your own home. A rhubarb patch, raspberry bushes, and a peach tree in the far corner, were mixed in with rose bushes. My grandmother canned peaches, applesauce and rhubarb sauce to eat all winter. The last thing that was added to his beautiful yard, nestled in the far right corner, was a round 18-foot above ground swimming pool.

I was the one placed in charge of pool maintenance and since we were out there, I decided to take a look. The bottom needed to be vacuumed since there were so many trees. It seemed like an endless battle. I asked Juan if he minded and he said, "No problem, go ahead." He and Doris were seated at the patio set having a beer and chatting, so he was occupied. I didn't want to come across as a rude American.

I grabbed the 30 feet of hose from the tool shed/pool house and quickly attached the vacuum head to the skimmer, turned on the switch and we had suction. It was a tedious job, slow movement of the vacuum head along the pool bottom to ensure a good seal and not cause too much turbulence. The worse thing to do was to displace the leaves and dirt into the water and not be able to suck it all out. Then after the task was completed and the water settled, it was as dirty as when you started.

I was vacuuming away and trying to be part of the conversation when Juan asked if he could help. He told us about his pool and its automatic vacuum system. They would toss this flat type robot vacuum cleaner into the pool's shallow end and it just moved along the bottom until it was perfectly cleaned. There was a special hook to retrieve the device from the bottom once it was complete. Doris and I share the trait that we are not mechanically inclined, so we both found this concept of a machine cleaning all by itself hard to grasp. I found myself wondering if my father might have been correct this time and this stray was a nut case.

It was starting to get dark and we all had to be to work early, so Juan agreed to let me drive him home. He was a perfect gentleman and we made plans to go to a movie over the weekend. He came to our house a few more times over the summer for dinner and Doris kept feeding him at lunchtime. There was never anything more than friendship between us, and the reason was because he smoked. There was just something about kissing someone who smoked, I couldn't do it. I enjoyed our conversations and we had fun going to the movies, but he wasn't my type.

When the summer ended, I returned to nursing school and on Monday morning Juan didn't show up for work. Doris was in her office starting her Monday morning ritual of doing the payroll, when a man appeared at her window. She was about to ask if she could help him when she realized he looked familiar. There stood Juan in an Italian, charcoal, pinstripe suit, starched white shirt and silk tie. He had a gold watch on his wrist and there was not a hair out of place. Who was this impersonator? What had he done with the laborer who lived in a rooming house? It was one of those few times in her life that my mother was speechless.

Her boss heard the familiar voice and once again escorted him into his office and closed the door. It was déjà vu. Doris sat at her desk unable to concentrate until she had the answers to this mystery. Then the door between the rooms opened and Juan emerged.

He walked the short distance to her desk where she was seated and unable to stand up. Doris looked up, "Who are you?" she asked. In perfect English he said, "My name is Juan Miguel Batista, and I am from Barcelona, Spain. My father owns many cattle ranches in Spain and South America, and he is one of your boss's leather suppliers." He explained that he was the eldest son and would be taking over the business and this was part of his training. His father had started from nothing as a gaucho on a ranch and now he owned them all. Juan's father had given him the best business university education and now was the time to complete his life education. His father wanted his children to appreciate the material things they had and never take for granted the people who worked for him making his life of entitlement possible.

Doris had been right from the beginning; he was one of her bosses rich friend's kids, working for the summer to see how real people live. Juan took out his leather billfold and pulled out his business card. He wrote his private phone number and said, "Doris, if you or any of your family are ever in Barcelona, call me and you will be a guest of mine at my villa." Now all the talk about the pool robot began to make sense. He wasn't a crazy homeless laborer. He was a wealthy Spanish cattle rancher.

Juan had come back to the office that day to say goodbye to Doris. In the beginning, he had thought she knew who he was and was giving him lunch because the boss told her to. When he found out that she was feeding him because she thought he was alone, living in a rooming house, he was shocked. He had been used to people trying to get material things from him and he couldn't believe that this woman didn't want anything. Doris just cared about him as a human being. He gave her a bear hug and again his sincere thanks for taking care of him while he was in Peabody and for sharing her family with him.

To this day, Doris makes jokes about why didn't I fall in love with Juan. I could have been rich, living on the coast of Spain with everything money could buy. Today I'm happy living on the coast of Massachusetts, with my wonderful husband and two beautiful daughters and I have everything that money CAN'T buy.

When I met my husband in 1980, my mother would have described his financial situation as, "A man who didn't have a pot to piss in or a window to throw it out of." Together we have worked hard, remodeled our entire home down to the studs, and created a close, loving family with our two beautiful daughters. Material things mean nothing to me. I have a philosophy I try to use with my childrens. I make them answer these three questions before they buy anything. Do I want it or do I really need it? If I really need it, will I die if I don't get it? If I will die if I don't get it, then buy it! In essence, as human beings, we need very few material things in this life to stay alive. Also, as human beings, one thing we cannot live without and have to have or we will most definitely die is love, and it's free.

Doris The Super Neighbor

Doris lived her entire life in a two-family house in Peabody, Massachusetts. The neighborhood was made up of stable long time residents like Doris, residing in single family homes on the odd-numbered side of the street. The even side was comprised of three family homes with transient tenants in and out. The strange part is that it was that way in the 1960's and 1970's, when I was growing up, and it continues to be that way today.

The neighbor on the left is one of Doris' many cousins and has lived there since he was five years old in one of the few one-family homes. He took over the family homestead in 1945 after he got married and never left. The neighbor on the right has also been there as long as Doris. Mary moved in as a child, and being the only girl in her family, stayed to care for her elderly parents. After her parents' death, she continued to live there in the first-floor apartment with her husband.

The other side of the street was another story. There was a three-family directly across from our house and it had seen young couples come and go. It had mocha brown, asbestos shingles and a long, narrow driveway that wrapped around to the back. Bordering the house was a vacant lot, and in 1969's the owners built a custom one-family home to live in and continued to rent the three apartments next door. The cozy four-room apartment on the top floor, had slanted ceilings and Doris used to refer to it as the dollhouse apartment for young newlyweds.

During the 60's, the standard was for people to get married a lot younger than they do today. Lots of couples were high school sweethearts and married soon after graduation. If you didn't get married right away, you lived with your parents paying room and board. There was not a mad rush to get your own place.

Going to college was not the norm, especially for girls. If a girl did continue on, it was as a teacher, secretary or nurse. Couples were becoming parents at a younger age, having their first baby before the age of 20 years old. Women were still stay at home moms and the term was "housewife." I'm not sure if the term "domestic engineer" had been coined yet. Taking care of the home and children was their profession and they did it with pride.

Doris was never the norm. She married at the ripe old age of 25 and had completed a two-year college program. She suffered infertility problems and couldn't get pregnant. My older brother wasn't adopted until Doris was already 30 years old, making her an old mother. My mother gave birth to me at 33 years old, only 10 days before her 34th birthday. My younger brother arrived just shy of the big number 40. While Doris was just becoming a mother and starting her family, her friends were done having their children.

The Newlyweds

One day a young couple moved into the second-floor apartment in the famous 3-family across the street. Jenny had married her high school sweetheart and had moved to the North Shore so her husband could start a new job in Boston. She had no relatives in the area and was very lonely, and then came Doris.

Doris' hair was already turning gray in her late 20's. I don't actually have any recollections of my mother's hair when it wasn't at least salt-and-pepper colored. She wore it very short, and with her natural curls, it always gave the impression she had just stepped out of a beauty salon after having a perm. This gave her the look of wisdom and I felt a look of being older than everyone else's mother. It was this look that had all the young wives and mothers of the neighborhood seeking help and advice from Doris.

Doris would see them coming in and out and would introduce herself, and it was instant friendship. It was safe to say that most days Doris was part of their daily routine. They were all stay-at-home moms or moms to be, so they took turns hosting afternoon coffees while the kids played in the yards. Doris was an adult to talk to and have fun with. They were trying to learn how to be good parents to their children, when they were not more than children themselves.

Unfortunately, there wasn't a course that you could take that gave all the answers. The only childcare book that was available was Dr. Spock. My mother never read instructions on how to do anything before she had kids. Why would she start now? She raised her children using the Doris Brown method. She taught right from wrong and that every action has a consequence. Those consequences could involve a physical spanking if warranted. It taught us at a young age that if we did something bad, we had better be willing to take the punishment that went with the action. Doris also had a unique way of teaching us to make decisions. She would ask us if we wanted to go to bed now or in 10 minutes and we would decide. She would never ask when we wanted to go to bed or the answer would have been never. It was always a choice between two things and even a three-year-old could decide.

Doris was always teaching. She just didn't know it. There were different life skill courses. She would teach the basics of childcare, such as taking a rectal temperature on a baby who had a fever. She shared some of her old-fashioned remedies for colic and teething pain. Today, she would have been arrested for rubbing whiskey on the baby's gums. Putting a stainless steel spoon in the freezer for the baby to chew on, once frozen, was more accepted.

Cooking was a given for Doris. In those days, wives' jobs included a meal on the table when the husband, the man of the house, got home from work. Most of these young girls didn't have enough time to learn from their mothers before they went out on their own. Doris would start with basic and inexpensive meals that were nutritious and simple to prepare.

Jenny was tall and willowy with sky blue eyes and natural blonde hair. She was the polar opposite of Doris in looks. She had just become a new mother to a beautiful baby girl with her mother's fair complexion and blue eyes. Under Doris' guidance, she was doing great with the baby, but her culinary skills were sadly lacking.

Doris decided that operation "Teach Jenny to Cook" was a number one priority. Her in-laws were coming in a month for the christening, and Jenny wanted to impress them. My mother decided to start with homemade macaroni and cheese. It was the concept of making a roux, which was the basis for many other meals, including sauces and gravies, and a simple place to start.

Doris arrived one afternoon at Jenny's apartment and said, "Have no fear, Doris is here." I think she had watched too many Mighty Mouse cartoons with us on Saturday mornings. This levity only seemed to make her more nervous. Jenny had purchased all the ingredients for the meal, and she watched and listened as Doris prepared the cheese sauce. Melt the butter in a medium saucepan, then whisk in 2–3 tablespoons of flour until you have a paste. Then slowly mix in the 1–2 cups of whole milk and as it comes to a slow boil, add grated or cubed cheeses of your choice. She had purchased sharp cheddar, which was her husband's favorite. Once it is melted, pour onto elbow macaroni and bake at 350 degrees for 45 minutes until browned.

My mother felt that since the meal was almost finished that she would leave the rest to Jenny and build her confidence. Later that night, around 5:30 there was a phone call while we were eating our supper. In the 60's, no one called at dinnertime unless there was an emergency or death. This was before anyone became obsessed with telephones, cell phones and the world of the annoying telemarketers.

It was Jenny and she was crying hysterically. Poor Doris couldn't make out what she was trying to say and she could hear her husband in the background trying to calm her down. Jenny whimpered, "The cheese is crunchy, it's hard and crunchy. What went wrong?" Doris paused for a minute to think what could have happened; no, she couldn't have been that dumb. Doris tried to keep her voice as sweet and nonjudgmental as possible and asked, "Jenny, honey, did you boil the macaroni before you poured the cheese sauce on it?" There was silence and then Jenny replied, "I am so stupid. How can you stand me? I can't even boil macaroni. I'm hopeless."

From that day forward, Doris included on any and every recipe that she wrote that involved a macaroni product, whether it was lasagna noodles or elbows, "Boil the macaroni product as instructed on the package label." I give Doris credit; she kept working with Jenny to make her an adequate cook so that the meals she made in the future would be edible. When it came to the meal for the christening, they all agreed that it might be above her ability at that time, so Doris catered it instead.

A few years and three kids later, Jenny and her husband had moved to an upscale new development a few towns over. The houses were all custom built split-levels and colonials and they all had attached two car garages, which was really a big deal in the late 60's. What was even more amazing was that they all had a front yard with impeccable green lawns and landscaping. The split entry had a long, serpentine-bricked walkway from the sidewalk leading to the formal front door. These houses were mansions compared to the multi-family houses that made up our neighborhood.

Jenny and her husband hadn't been gone very long when Doris received a written invitation to a house-warming, cocktail party, at their new home. I had never seen Doris so nervous about going to a party. I could tell that she felt Jenny's new neighbors, doctors and lawyers, were out of her league. The bigger problem was what could she buy for a house warming gift. Money was limited and Jenny had such modern taste with a lot of sleek, teak wood furniture. Doris didn't know where to start. Our houses furnishings were purchased around 1949 when Doris got married, and they were solid maple wood, in what she referred to as early depression style.

Doris decided to start with the gift. She had always been crafty and could create things out of nothing and a little cash. The only problem was that sometimes you could not identify what she had actually created. Doris remembered that she had an odd-shaped piece of driftwood in the basement, so that is where she began.

What could she make out of this piece of wood that looked like a set of small deer antlers? It was 24 inches long at the base, and the ends uniformly curved up another eight inches with small appendages to give it some interest. There was a natural bowl shape in the center of the base and it suddenly came to her: a centerpiece for the new dining room buffet. I asked her again, because I didn't think I heard her correctly the first time. "Mom, you are going to make a what? For there what? Made out of what?" Once again I thought that Doris had truly lost her mind.

She remembered that there could be bugs in the wood so she started by having it sandblasted at a woodworking shop for only 2 dollars. Doris did what she did best: cleaned the wood with mineral spirits; rubbed a coating of cordovan shoe polish into the wood to bring out all the grain; linseed oil for a hand rubbed finish that was beautiful and would protect the wood forever from cracking. She bought two brass-like metal candleholders and screwed them symmetrically on either side of the bowl-like base. She placed some realistic plastic fruit, if there is such a thing, into the natural wooden bowl. Finally, she added tapered, orchid candles in the holders to match the color scheme. Once again with some ingenuity and imagination, my mother took a piece of wood she found on a beach in Maine and turned it into a piece of modern art. Jenny truly loved this unique piece, but more important was the fact that Doris had taken the time and love to make something so perfect just for her. The driftwood centerpiece still remains on the same buffet in the same dining room with some minor changes to the fruit and candles over the years.

Doris had the problem of the gift solved. The new dilemma was what would she wear? She couldn't afford to buy a new outfit, and what does one wear to a cocktail party. She decided to create herself something. It was very secretive. All week she cut and sewed in the privacy of her bedroom. The Saturday night of the party arrived and the long wait was over as Doris unveiled the cocktail party outfit. We had all gathered in the kitchen as Doris came out of her room, down the short hall to where we were waiting.

I heard the gasp from my father before I actually saw her. My mother was wearing a maternity smock. Doris had worn her good black pedal pusher slacks and black flat leather sandals and on top she was pregnant. She had sewed a white sailor blouse, sleeveless, trimmed in black gaugrain ribbons around the V-neck and on the sailor collar. At first I thought I was hallucinating. She had a flat stomach that afternoon and now she was seven months pregnant. The desired effect was achieved by using a small bed pillow that she had altered for an authentic look. Doris was afraid that she was not going to have anything to talk to these people about and being pregnant would at least be a conversation starter. Doris knew people and she knew from experience that people couldn't resist a pregnant woman.

Doris walked into the party and her friend Jenny saw her and almost fainted. Doris explained her reasoning to Jenny, the person who forgot to cook the macaroni before she added the cheese, and she found Doris' explanation perfectly logical. My mother found a comfortable place to sit and almost immediately everyone came over to say hello. People asked when she was due. Others wanted to know if it was her first baby? These highly educated people acted just as Doris predicted they would. The shock only lasted a few minutes when she admitted she wasn't pregnant and had done it to have something to talk about. It worked because she started telling jokes and had everyone laughing. Only Doris would think up an idea to make believe she was pregnant to hide her insecurity. Once again she was in her element using herself to make people laugh.

The Marriage Counselor

All the couples that lived on my mother's street were not as happy as Jenny and her husband. My mother had a young friend named Olivia and she was more like the baby sister Doris never had. When she was about to get married, she and her fiancé purchased a house down the street from Doris. I think that she felt secure around my mother; she had just turned 18 years old and was getting married in a few months. Everything was going great or it appeared to be at that time. Doris volunteered her talents and helped Olivia apply fresh paint to all the walls and ceilings, make curtains for all the windows and turned her first floor apartment into a dream house before they got married.

Olivia had planned a beautiful formal wedding. All her friends were young and single, and she wanted Doris to be part of her wedding. Being twice the age of the wedding party she declined, feeling that she was too old. Olivia was upset because Doris was a good friend so they reached a compromise and she had to settle for me as her flower girl.

It was a summer rainbow wedding and all the bridesmaids were in knee-length pastel dresses, in yellow, pink, orchid, and blue with sashes around their waists, tied into bows at the back. They all wore three-inch high-heeled shoes with pointed toes, dyed to match their dresses. Everyone wore a headpiece that matched the color of their dress, and I was the exception with tiny white daises on mine

I was four years old when I was the flower girl at Olivia's wedding. My mother created my beautiful dress. I was already a bit of a chubette with light brown shoulder length curls, uneven bangs and rosy cheeks. To flatter my figure, Doris made my dress out of a pale pink almost white organza, a full skirt and short puffed sleeves. There were three flower appliqués down the center of the bodice. It had a darker pink sash that went around my waist and tied into a bow at the back. I can still remember the lace on my white ankle socks and how proud I was of my new white patent leather shoes.

The wedding was beautiful and after the honeymoon they moved into the apartment as husband and wife. They made a beautiful couple; they were both short of stature and had dark eyes and hair. They looked as though they had been made for each other. After a few years a problem arose and Olivia couldn't get pregnant. I remember her sitting at our kitchen table crying because another month had gone by and still she wasn't pregnant.

Doris had compassion, having gone through her own struggles to have children, so she tried to help and encourage Olivia by reminding her that she had proven all the doctors wrong.

I didn't understand what was happening at the time, but their marriage had many other issues. On a fall night, after dark, while we were sitting in the parlor watching television, someone ran onto our front porch. My mother got up from the sofa and looked out the window to see who it was. There was banging on the front door and cries for help, "Let me in, please let me in." It was Olivia and she was crying. Doris opened the door, pulled her into the front hall, then slammed the door closed and double locked it. Next thing I knew Doris was running to the back door and the basement to assure all the doors were secured. Doris had that same look of fear I had seen on her face the night her cousin Alicia's husband came after her, threatening to kill her. I had never seen a person so terrified before, and there it was again on Olivia's face.

Doris stopped long enough to take a good look at Olivia. Her right eye was black and blue and swollen shut. Her upper lip was split in the center and she had bright red blood trickling down her chin. The front of her blouse was torn and there were bruises starting to form around her neck. "What did he do to you?" Doris asked.

Olivia sat down on a kitchen chair, trying to stop crying as her body continued to shudder. Doris had already prepared two bags of ice for her eye and lip, which continued to swell. Doris was a loyal friend and confidant and any secret you trusted to her would never be exposed. Olivia apparently had a secret about her husband that was too painful to even trust my mother.

Olivia's perfect husband was drinking and physically abusing her on a regular basis. He was taking out all of his frustration on her tiny, five foot two inch frame. Why couldn't he get her pregnant? Was there something wrong with his manhood? Why did he keep getting bypassed for promotions at work? Why didn't she make him happy anymore? He had come home after drinking at the neighborhood bar, was drunk and started using her for a punching bag. He had never hit her this hard and never in her face. Prior to this night, it had always been where it wouldn't show to the public. Her husband had pulled her hair, kicked her in the lower legs and punched her in the abdomen and back. Then tonight something changed. He grabbed her around the neck and squeezed. Olivia feared this time he was going to strangle her to death. There was blankness in his eyes as she pleaded for him to stop. It was as though he was looking right through her, in a trance.

Suddenly there was someone at our front door and he was banging with his fists and yelling, "Open the God damn door now! Doris, open the door or I'll kill you both." I was so scared. I saw my mother give a signal to my grandmother who had come down to our apartment when the banging started. Teodolinda, grabbed my younger brother and me by the arms and ran with us to the second floor and locked the door. My grandmother was praying in Portuguese and I knew it wasn't good. I started to pray out loud, "Please God, don't let him hurt my mother. Please help her."

Doris knew that the only thing that was keeping them alive was that door, and she wasn't about to open it. She ran to the phone and called the police. It seemed like hours before the siren could be heard and they had Olivia's husband in handcuffs. He was arrested for drunk and disorderly conduct. This man had tried to kill his wife, threatened to kill my mother and that was it. In the 1960's there was no domestic abuse legislation. It was still the norm that a wife was a piece of property and the husband was the one with all the power. His family bailed him out of jail, and he was back in their apartment the next day.

Olivia was lost, scared and didn't know where to turn. Her own family were immigrants who also held the beliefs that a wife had to be obedient to her husband. Doris had seen first hand what a weak, domineering, and jealous man is capable of doing to a woman. In this case, he could and probably would kill her if she didn't leave him. My mother felt that any man who raises a hand to a woman or child is a lowlife, the lowest animal on the food chain. Doris encouraged Olivia to contact her friend who was an attorney, and get a restraining order and leave her husband. Olivia was afraid of him and followed Doris' advice. She had him served with the restraining order and was able to move into a small apartment of her own.

As time went on, Olivia's memory of abuse started to fade. She forgot the handprints around her neck that night in Doris' front hall. She called her friend Doris to say she had changed her mind. She had been seeing her husband; he was sorry and promised not to hit her anymore. They were going to adopt a baby and start a new family and life together. She still loved him.

Doris knew from her experiences that a leopard never changes his spots. Olivia moved back into the house she had shared with her husband. My mother knew about her husband's family and their history of mental illness and alcoholism. Olivia's husband had a lot of emotional issues to work through and without professional help she was confident he would repeat his abuse. It was only a question of time, when would it happen and how serious would it be the next time. This reconciliation, new baby, and perfect family was only a fantasy that would never work.

Doris had a saying that she would use: "Fool me once, shame on you. Fool me twice, shame on me." Throughout her life, this saying was the criteria that she used to nominate someone to be placed on the "Doris Brown Shit List." This was a prestigious list that a select few people where placed on over her lifetime. Doris was not quick to place someone on it, but be warned, once on the list, you never got off. It took work for someone to take Doris' friendship, generosity, and loyalty and turn it around and betray her and take advantage of her in some way.

With Olivia, Doris respected her decision and continued to be there for her as her friend, never judging. Things changed after she went back to her husband. He wouldn't let Doris come to their house. He was more controlling of her activities. Her husband blamed Doris for his wife leaving him and not the fact that he had tried to strangle her. One night, Olivia was once again on our porch, with a split lip and looking for help. Doris was big on helping people only if they were willing to help themselves.

Olivia spent the night and Doris spelled it out for her. My mother was not willing to have this man disrupt her life anymore. She wasn't going to subject her children or herself to his threats of violence. She did not choose to have him in her life, and she had her own problems with my father. She gave Olivia a choice: either she left him and started a new life away from the abuse or Doris would have to sever their friendship. She knew that Olivia wasn't ready to make a change and would stay in her abusive relationship. Doris knew because she was still married to my father with his verbal abuse and couldn't leave her marriage until she could become financially secure and able to care for her children.

We never heard from Olivia again; after that morning she left our kitchen and told Doris her decision was to stay with him. Olivia lived with her husband for another five years. She was able to adopt a beautiful baby, so one part of her dream had come true. There were episodes during those last five years when the police were called to their home, and a few times her husband was taken away in handcuffs.

Over the years, my mother would wave hello if she passed Olivia on the street, but they hadn't spoken. It had been 15 years after her divorce when Olivia bumped into my mother at a local department store and they started to talk. They had both remarried and found nice husbands the second time around.

Their children were all married, and Doris had finally become a grandmother. It was a pleasant exchange, only Doris has a long memory. Once a charter club member of the "Shit List," you can never totally get your name removed.

It is amazing to me that 40 years later and we have made such small strides in the area of domestic abuse. The only change in the law is that police officers are mandated to arrest for assault and battery and not just disorderly conduct when they respond to a domestic abuse call and there is visual, physical evidence of abuse. There are more non-profit groups, such as HAWC, in our area that help women trapped in these relationships to seek safe housing, counseling, and legal assistance.

I am grateful every day that my mother instilled in me over the years, by her example and verbally, a few important life lessons. Doris would say these things over and over again until it became part of who I am.

- You are a strong person and can be anything you want if you get an education.
- You can be financially independent and you don't need a man to take care of you.
- You never need to have a man in your life to be complete.
- You choose to have a man in your life because you love him and marriage is always a choice, not a necessity.

The Barber

If they had held a contest for the best neighbor in the world, Doris would have won without a doubt. She was always there to listen to a problem and give a needed hug. Doris would do anything that anyone asked. In some cases, you actually didn't have to ask; if she felt you needed it, she just did it on her own. The only thing she refused to do, and everyone knew it, was to clean houses. The chore she dreaded the most was washing dishes. Otherwise, if it was legal, she was game.

If you needed cooking lessons, that was no problem. If you were a disaster in the kitchen, she would cater the meal for the in-laws and let you take all the credit. She used to joke that it was only a little white lie, plus she couldn't stand by and let innocent people be poisoned even if it was a mother-in-law. The older ladies in the neighborhood didn't drive, but that wasn't a problem for Doris. Thursday was grocery day. Everyone was loaded into the station wagon and off they went to the First National grocery store. When we returned home, all the groceries were carried into the houses and put on the kitchen tables. One of the women, Millie, was thin and frail and would get short of breath after any exertion. Due to her heart condition she couldn't lift anything so the door-to-door delivery became a tradition. What was good for one lady was good for all.

The First National was the catalyst for the creation of the "Hopeless Chest," as my brothers affectionately named it. It is a tradition for nice Portuguese girls to make things, crocheted or knitted, to store in a special cedar-lined Hope Chest in preparation for the day when you would eventually get married. Like my mother, I felt crocheting bureau scarves was impractical so we started buying things instead.

At that time, The First National ran a promotion; for every $5 spent on groceries, you could buy a single piece of stainless flatware, such as knife or salad fork, for a nickel. Since the ladies we took shopping didn't need flatware, I collected and used their receipts every week. Using my babysitting money, I was able to buy a 5-piece place setting of quality stainless flatware for the bargain price of $0.25. I acquired my first and only set of stainless flatware for 12 using this method and still use it today. It is a modern pattern with long sleek handles and a brushed metal finish.

It was at First National that I started my love relationship with green stamps. When you checked out, there was a small machine next to the cash register and it would spew out a four-inch wide strip of stamps based on the amount of money you spent. These green postage-like stamps with $ signs in the centers were collected every week, carefully pasted on both sides of the pages in a special 4×6 inch book. The goal was to fill as many books so they could be redeemed as currency at the nearby redemption center.

The redemption center was a single-story, cement block building only five miles away from my house. Aside from a large sign hung over the single glass panel door on the front façade, there were no other windows or indication of what the building was used for. It was filled with wonderful kitchen things for the Hopeless Chest. Over the years I was able to buy my service of 12 Corell dishes in a dainty blue snowflake pattern. Since my grandmother and neighbors also contributed to the hopeless chest fund, I bought fifteen different Corning Ware casseroles in various sizes and shapes in the original blue design. Like all things that are too good to be true, the green stamps came to an end and The First National food chain went bankrupt.

Doris started to branch out trying to help the neighbors save money. All the families were living on one income, and the majority of the fathers were blue-collar workers, such as truck drivers, car mechanics, and factory laborers. Everyday was a struggle to make ends meet. She got it into her head that she could save everyone so much money if she purchased her own electric hair clippers and gave all the boys in the neighborhood their haircuts.

This was still in the early 1960's and the Beatles had not come over the pond just yet. Long hair was not the norm. Most young men got regular haircuts every 6–8 weeks to prevent the hair from ever reaching the top of the ear. The haircut that Doris proposed to learn was the ever-popular buzz cut, or as it was affectionately called, the whiffel. Doris had been present enough times when the neighborhood barber had performed his magic on her sons to know how it was done. How hard could it be? Those five words would become a mantra that would come back to haunt her over the years.

She planned to buy a six-inch long electric device, with two rows of very sharp blades, that vibrated back and forth so quickly that the hair was removed instantly. What did she propose to do with this lethal weapon? Doris was going to take the clippers in her steady hand, gently run the blades over the child's scalp, until barely ⅛ inch of soft downy hair remained.

Once again Doris' impulsiveness took over and she purchased the electric clipper set. There were actually a few different attachments for shaving the back of the neck and sideburns. It came with a 20-page instruction booklet to explain the different cutting techniques, hair textures, cowlicks and hair growth patterns. Then there was the warning typed in red print: "This device, if used improperly, can cause serious injury and or death." I could see a problem even if Doris couldn't. A young boy sitting on a step stool in the garage, one low wattage overhead light bulb for lighting, and he makes a sudden move. One slip of Doris' hand and we have a lacerated jugular vein or carotid artery in the neck and the results, one dead child.

I feared for the life of every boy in the neighborhood. I had already been Doris' victim. She masqueraded as a beautician for years, cutting my hair and trimming my bangs, and it wasn't pretty. I have pictures as a child and my light brown bangs go up and down like a picket fence. Other times in her attempt to get them even, she kept going shorter and shorter until there were wisps of hair sticking straight out from my hairline. I was so emotionally traumatized that from the age of five on, I never let her cut my hair again. I wore my hair long, grew out my bangs, and have never had bangs since. Over the years when a hair stylist suggests we try bangs, I get myself a new stylist and I'm 50 plus years old.

The dilemma was how to stop Doris from becoming the neighborhood barber. Unfortunately in those days you didn't even need formal training or a license from the state. You just needed a comb, scissors and clippers. My mother had enough sense to experiment on my brothers before she attempted the neighbors' children. My poor older brother became her first victim.

One sunny morning, the week after school recessed for the summer, my mother set up the Doris Brown garage/barber shop. Her son was her first unwilling victim. My older brother's hair was a dark chestnut brown, thin and board straight. He had taken his T-shirt off to prevent the hair from sticking and causing itching later in the day. She guided him onto the step stool, which she had already placed directly under the only overhead light bulb in the garage. Next she wrapped an old white sheet around his neck and tied it in place.

What happened next was right out of a horror film. Doris combed Junior's hair forward over his eyes and proceeded to plug the clippers into the only wall outlet. It was like being in the dentist's chair when he turns on the drill and you say a silent prayer that the Novocain has already taken effect. Junior couldn't see! Doris had covered his eyes and all he could hear was the buzzing sound of the clippers getting closer and closer.

Doris had seen our barber enough that she knew to start at the base of the scalp and use a clean smooth movement from back to front. What she had failed to learn was when a child's hair was as long as Junior's, the real barber would cut it shorter before he started. If you don't, the longer hair has a tendency to catch in the clipper and it pulls the hair out at the root. It only took the first pass for Doris to realize this as my brother let out a blood-curdling scream as the hair in the center of his scalp was ripped out, not shaved. Now Junior was off the stool and refusing to let Doris at him for a second pass. Doris turned off the clippers and tried to reason with him. The problem was he had a jagged racing stripe down the center of his head. She might have left it if he didn't look like an escapee from an insane asylum.

I couldn't watch anymore. I ran into the quiet of the house. I'm not sure how she convinced Junior to let her finish, but I am sure a bribe was involved. Doris took a pair of scissors and cut off all of his excess hair and started again. Once she made the second pass in the same area, she actually didn't hurt him, there were no screams. Doris was off and running. She wanted to do more because it was actually fun. My mother had given him a descent buzz cut for her first haircut. It took a few extra runs over his scalp to make the hair even in length and she only gave him one nick that was barely visible. Next was my baby brother and she did another great job. They were immediately sent out into the neighborhood to play and let their friends know she was open for business.

Doris used her sons as a live advertisement. I say live because it showed her talent as a barber and the fact they lived through it with no accidental cutting of any major arteries. My mother continued to cut the boys' hair in the neighborhood every summer until the buzz cut was out of style. Once the age of rock and roll hit America and long hair and bangs were in, she lost her loyal cliental. I wonder if it could have been partly my fault since I did show them all my baby pictures and the bangs and asked, "Do you really want my mother cutting your bangs?" Doris was never allowed near anyone's head Again.

Epilogue

This book was a glimpse of what it was like living and growing up with my mother, Doris. The many sides of her personality and the love and caring that always came through, no matter what she attempted over her 80+ years.

Doris continues to live in the same house that I grew up in. She continues to drive her 2002 Hyundai two door sedan, but only during daylight hours and on back streets. Every morning, Monday through Friday, weather-permitting, she walks at least 1–3 miles a day. Her routes always change and there is always a pit stop at the Peabody Senior Citizen (Center) as Doris refers to it.

Most of Doris' close friends have passed away in the last few years and those that are still alive have multiple medical problems. She is probably in the best overall physical condition, so she does the chauffeuring and home deliveries of her special cooking. One thing Doris has never stopped or even slowed down on is her cooking. Every few week she prepares a few dishes for my brothers and me. Her top choices are our family's favorites: boneless fried chicken, beef stew, and chicken and rice.

She recently started to cook monthly for the cloistered sisters of the Carmelite. It is her way to say thank you for all the prayers that they say for Doris and her family. This new endeavor has taken her cooking down a new path. The nuns are vegetarians, so Doris has been experimenting on adapting her signature dishes for their enjoyment using fish. How does macaroni and cheese with shrimp grab you? Maybe the nuns' favorite, Shepherd pie using salmon instead of ground beef. I am sure there will be a new cook book in there somewhere.

Since Doris has become health conscious, she cooks with olive oil and low saturated fats. There are no more organ meats or liver. She prefers lean cuts of beef, and fishes high in Omega 3 vitamins. Her bread making is now along the whole grain varieties. The only exception to the rule is her Portuguese Sweet Bread and there she doesn't spare the butter and sugar the recipe calls for. The bread is a treat for special holidays.

Her three children and six grandchildren are still the center of her life. Doris attends all of their plays, dance recitals and sporting events. Just recently she had the pleasure of witnessing her first granddaughter graduate from the prestigious Smith College in North Hampton, Massachusetts. By the time the granddaughters arrived, four in all, she said they could be anything they wanted. No longer did she limit a woman's choices to nurse or teacher. Her oldest granddaughter received a Bachelor of Science degree in Engineering Science. Her second granddaughter wants to be the next Katie Couric, while the third and fourth granddaughters are in college, aiming to become thespians and singers. There is no stopping the next generation of Brown/Breen women, and God willing there is no stopping Doris for many years to come.

THE END

23272653R00139